THEN

The Club met in a rented mansion on Fourth and A Street and had 92 Members, and a steak dinner cost just 35 cents. That worked until 1916 when a four-story Spanish-style structure was designed by Member architects, Hebbard and Winslow. The building was constructed at 1333 Seventh Avenue and included a lounge to serve Members with ladies or ladies alone—this was called the Luce Women's room, after founding member, Edgar Luce. The estimated cost for the building was $29,000. Annual dues were raised to $30 and non-residents were now required to pay a $15 membership fee.

NOW

Today, The University Club crowns Symphony Towers as one (if not the) highest point in San Diego, and boasts unparalleled views of San Diego and the bay. After the $2.4 million dollar renovation and expansion in 2010, Members enjoy arguably the best views of their city, and many consider the Club to be the premier social and business venue in the city—open only to Members and their guests.

THEN

A highlight of the University Club was its Friday noon luncheon programs. The participants were people of "local and national eminence who reflected the broad gamut of human experience."

NOW

Today, the Club's Business Alliance presents the Distinguished Speaker Series breakfast (monthly on Friday) featuring informative, stimulating topics delivered by diverse, qualified, influential and interesting speakers. Continuing with the time honored traditions of the past but always seeking to be contemporary, the University Club continues to be on the cutting edge of business and social clubs.

Circle of Excellence

2011: University Club Awarded 2010 Gold Circle of Excellence Award by ClubCorp

The University Club has been honored with the 2010 Gold Circle of Excellence award by ClubCorp, the world leader in delivering premier golf, private club and resort experiences. The Gold Circle of Excellence award is ClubCorp's most prestigious performance recognition award and The University Club atop Symphony Towers was the only club in the Business & Sports Clubs division to receive this honor.

ClubCorp awards the Gold Circle of Excellence annually to clubs based upon achievement of specific objectives and performance goals. The Gold Circle of Excellence criteria focuses on key business initiatives, including Membership, Member retention, operations and efficiency.

"We are very honored and proud, and simply think that this award is a direct reflection of our great membership here at The University Club." – Frank Polinski, Director of Food and Beverage

1951: Jack in the Box opens its first restaurant in San Diego

1930 City of San Diego population is 147,995. San Diego County population is 209,659.

1940 Morgan Eastman explains the "X-Ray of Motion" at University Club's famous Friday luncheon.

1951 Jack in the Box gets its start. Robert O. Peterson opens first drive-through restaurant at 63rd St. and El Cajon Boulevard.

1954 San Diego's new Public Library opens. University of San Diego founded in Linda Vista.

1956 General Dynamics takes over Convair. Campus in San Diego's La Jolla area is proposed for a University of California site.

1964 Sea World opens in Mission Bay Park

1969 San Diego – Coronado Bay Bridge opens, replacing ferry service across San Diego Bay.

The Padres make their major league debut on April 8 with a 2-1 victory over Houston in front of 23,370 fans at San Diego Stadium.

1970 San Diego becomes California's second largest city, with a population of 696,474. San Diego County population is 1,357,854.

2000 City of San Diego population reaches 1,223,400. San Diego County population is 2,813,833.

1930	1940	1950	1960	1970	1980	1990 – 2000

1957: Robert Dedman (far right) founds ClubCorp.

1957 Robert Dedman founds ClubCorp, the University Club's future parent company and network of clubs.

1960 ClubCorp's grand opening of Brookhaven in Dallas, Texas. When opened, it's the largest golf club in the world.

1970 University Club's second Clubhouse completed. Three-story "modern" brick building erected on the corner of Seventh and A Streets.

1982 ClubCorp goes international, to bankers in Taiwan, and establishes Club Corporation of Asia, a joint venture company based in Hong Kong.

1985 University Club has 650 Members at the Seventh Ave. clubhouse location.

1989 University Club becomes a part of the ClubCorp family and moves into current home on the 34th floor penthouse of Symphony Towers.

1991 The University Club is selected and honored with the 'Club of the Year' award and recognition by the Club Corporation of America.

1999 Signature Gold established for Club Members to have complimentary dining and complimentary golf at affiliate clubs across the nation.

2002 Doug Wilson selected Chair of University Club Board of Directors.

2003 University Club storage room is converted into today's charming Wine Cellar and the Wine Program is established for Members' personalized wine storage lockers, savings on wine purchasing and enjoyment in the Club.

2005 Lamp of Learning Scholarship Foundation established at the University Club

2007 KSL Partners purchases ClubCorp and aligns resort properties such as Hotel Del Coronado, Rancho Las Palmas, La Costa Resort and Spa to family of clubs.

2008 ClubCorp operates 154 private clubs with 15,000 employees worldwide.

2009 University Club celebrates 100th anniversary with more than 2,400 individuals in membership.

2010 University Club undergoes $2.4 million reinvention, acquiring entire 34th Floor Penthouse of Symphony Towers.

Photo by Melissa Jacobs

To Duane
Enjoy reading about San Diego's
oldest private club!

WE GRATEFULLY ACKNOWLEDGE THE SUPPORT OF OUR SPONSORS:

Irvine Company Office Properties—Symphony Towers

ClubCorp Inc.—The University Club Atop Symphony Towers

1909 University Club of San Diego, Inc. Board of Directors

Robert A. McNeely and Delores A. McNeely
Jessie J. Knight Jr. and Joye Blount
Dan and Lisa Hom

A PICTORIAL HISTORY OF THE
UNIVERSITY CLUB OF
SAN DIEGO

By Julie M. Walke

Featuring Presidents' Biographies by San Diego Historian Richard W. Crawford

1909 University Club of San Diego Inc.

THE UNIVERSITY CLUB
ATOP SYMPHONY TOWERS

Front Cover: *Peden & Munk/Trunk Archive*

Back cover: Evening dining in the 1909 Founders Room is an elegant and sophisticated experience. Capped off by the musical sounds of world-renowned jazz pianist Mike Wofford. Wofford has been an accompanist and music director jazz singers Sarah Vaughn and Ella Fitzgerald among others. He has performed with many famous jazz and non-jazz greats since starting his career in the 1960s. *Peden & Munk/Trunk Archive*

Hardcover: *Photo by ZackBenson.com*

The 1909 University Club of San Diego, Inc.
PO Box 195
La Jolla, CA 92038

THE
DONNING COMPANY
PUBLISHERS

The Donning Company Publishers
184 Business Park Drive, Suite 206
Virginia Beach, VA 23462

Steve Mull, *General Manager*
Barbara B. Buchanan, *Office Manager*
Richard A. Horwege, *Senior Editor*
Stephanie Danko, *Graphic Designer*
Kathy Adams, *Imaging Artist*
Katie Gardner, *Project Research Coordinator*
Nathan Stufflebean, *Donning Research Supervisor*
Katie Gardner, *Marketing Assistant*

Steve Mull, *Project Director*

Library of Congress Cataloging-in-Publication Data

Data available at the Library of Congress.
ISBN: 978-1-57864-906-8

Printed in the USA at Walsworth Publishing Company

TABLE OF CONTENTS

8   ACKNOWLEDGMENTS

9   FOREWORD *by Bob McNeely, Chairman, Board of Governors, University Club Atop Symphony Towers*

10   CHAPTER ONE: **UNIVERSITY CLUB ATOP SYMPHONY TOWERS**
       ⚜ A Dynamic Club
       ⚜ The Renovation Leading to the Reinvention
       ⚜ A New Era
       ⚜ Clubs within the Club
       ⚜ Formation of the Board of Governors in 1989
       ⚜ Board of Governors Reinvented in 2012
       ⚜ Philanthropy
       ⚜ Lamp of Learning Scholarship Fund and Scholars and Committee
       ⚜ The Legacy Board: The 1909 University Club of San Diego, Inc., and the
          1909 University Club Board of Directors
       ⚜ Member Activities: Distinguished Speaker Series, Art Events, Young Executive Society (YES)
          All Aboard, and Cheese and Craft Beer Pairing
       ⚜ The University Club Atop Symphony Towers Team

46   CHAPTER TWO: **BUILD IT AND THEY WILL COME**
       ⚜ A Club with a History
       ⚜ A New Club on the Horizon
       ⚜ An Iconic Structure

64 CHAPTER THREE: **THE FORMATION OF THE 1909 UNIVERSITY CLUB OF SAN DIEGO, INC.**
- ☙ The University Club on Seventh Avenue, Circa 1984
- ☙ The Men's Glee—A Musical Tradition
- ☙ Storm Clouds Gathering
- ☙ The Opportunity of a Lifetime
- ☙ Symphony Towers Rises
- ☙ The 1909 Legacy Board Is Established
- ☙ The First Female President
- ☙ Establishing a Place in History

84 CHAPTER FOUR: **105 YEARS OF SAN DIEGO LEADERSHIP**
- ☙ Leaders Who Set the Mark: University Club Presidents 1909–2014
  Presidents' Biographies by San Diego Historian Richard W. Crawford

112 CHAPTER FIVE: **THE COLLEGE GRADUATE CLUB AND THE FOUNDING OF THE UNIVERSITY CLUB**
- ☙ The College Graduate Club of 1896
- ☙ Incorporation of the University Club in 1909

128 ABOUT THE AUTHORS

ACKNOWLEDGMENTS

I n this book, I endeavor to provide readers with not only the Club's history and traditions but also to illustrate how the University Club of San Diego has been an integral part of San Diego's social growth and economic development. To fully accomplish this, San Diego Historian Richard W. Crawford was asked to supply his expertise to research and write about the past Presidents of the University Club from its 1909 founding through the 1989 transition as the 1909 University Club of San Diego, Inc. A special acknowledgment and thank you goes to 1909 Board members Mike Bixler, Ann Beard, and Rob Scott who served on the Book Committee.

With the publishing of this book, the 1909 Board of Directors is fulfilling their mission to protect and enhance the legacy, traditions, and assets of the 1909 University Club of San Diego, Inc., while working with ClubCorp, Inc., and the larger membership of the University Club Atop Symphony Towers.

I would like to acknowledge the 1909 University Club of San Diego Board of Directors: Vice President Suzanne Swift; Secretary Robert G. Scott; Chief Financial Officer Don Fine; Board members Mike Bixler, Ann Beard, and Jim Alcorn; and Board member emeritus Phillip Gildred. This project would not have been possible without their financial and practical support. Special thanks to Jon Heller and Kendall DePascal.

My sincere gratitude goes to General Manager Matt Parsons and his team who spent many hours coordinating group photos and location shots. Thanks to Ed Nesfield, Lauren Scobel, Amy Mitchell, Laura Bull, and Brigette Bower. And, my personal thanks to Tommy Trause and Casey Falkner.

I am also appreciative for the enthusiasm and support from Robert "Bob" McNeely, Chairman of the Board of Governors at the Symphony Towers Club, and fellow Executive Committee members, especially Jeff Light, Linc Ward, and Dr. Jim Bowers. One evening Jeff Light was talking to Dr. Bowers and me. He marveled over our combined years of dedication to the Club. Light concluded his observation by saying, "Jim, you are the soul and Julie is the spirit of the Club." I couldn't have said it better.

Enjoy this book and keep it as a reminder that all of us carry forth a piece of San Diego history.

Julie M. Walke

FOREWORD

ike a fine aged wine, the University Club of San Diego has evolved over time and enjoys a rich history of involvement with the leadership of the San Diego community. Over the years, even dating back before its formation in 1896, the leadership of the Club has represented an outstanding cadre of individuals of prominence and influence in San Diego. The evolution of the Club has maintained a rich cultural history while embracing the growth and change that was and is San Diego today.

The Club has and continues to have a profound impact on the fabric of San Diego through the composition of its membership, many of whom have been and are corporate executives, business and community leaders. The Club has endeavored to include in its membership thought leaders, young and old, who bring a diverse perspective regarding the future of San Diego.

This book represents a chronology of history about the University Club, its importance to the San Diego region, and how it has grown over the years to be the Club it is today. You will learn about Club ownership and the philosophy of ClubCorp America. You will meet the University Club staff members who operationalize the mission of the Club and provide an excellent experience to members and their guests. Importantly, you will meet the founding members, men and women who provided a vision for the Club during its infancy, and see how that vision is responsible for the legacy of the Club we know today.

I would like to express my appreciation to Julie Walke, President of the 1909 University Club of San Diego, Inc., for her tireless efforts in making this book a reality; to Matt Parsons and his team for carrying on the tradition of an excellent Club experience to the membership; and, to an excellent Board of Governors for their time, energy, and enthusiasm on behalf of the Club membership to ensure the legacy of a wonderful experience for members.

On behalf of the University Club Board of Governors, I am proud to share this wonderful book with you.

Sincerely,
Robert A. McNeely
*Chairman,
Board of Governor's,
University Club Atop Symphony Towers*

"I am bullish regarding the future of the Club. We have a great representation of the leadership of San Diego who serve on our Board of Governors. We have provided opportunities for new members to become more involved with the leadership of our Club."

CHAPTER ONE

UNIVERSITY CLUB ATOP SYMPHONY TOWERS

M ost would agree that downtown San Diego is beautiful. Throughout the year, visitors and residents alike can see the sparkling bay view from Jacaranda-lined Ash Street heading downhill from Cortez Hill, through Little Italy and west to the San Diego Bay. They can watch the active vista of Harbor Drive winding south along the Marina District, passing the *Star of India*, the Cruise Ship Terminals, Broadway Pier, USS *Midway* Museum, Seaport Village, and the Convention Center. They can experience the vibrancy of the Gaslamp and East Village Districts, home to Petco Park, Ballpark Village, and the new Central Library with its iconic steel and mesh dome. Balboa Park, one of the nation's largest urban cultural parks, is to the north. Wherever one chooses to look, there is something for the eyes to appreciate about San Diego.

The most impressive of all is the skyline view above the Center City surrounded by San Diego Bay, Point Loma, Coronado Island, Mexico, and the Pacific Ocean. This is the view from San Diego's

finest private club, the University Club Atop Symphony Towers perched on the top of one of the city's tallest buildings.

First-time visitors may remark on the friendliness of the valet as they drop their car off at street level, or take note of the dramatic, symphony-themed mural that spans almost the entire length of the lobby—a welcoming entrance to the Jacobs Music Center and Copley Symphony Hall. But there is no way to prepare for the stunning views that awaits

one when stepping out of the elevator lobby and into this penthouse club. A wall of floor to ceiling windows beckons to the views beyond.

The uninitiated visitor gets an immediate impression of hipness rather than history, but on closer examination find it is a memorable and notable historic San Diego institution. Today members' activities and events follow some of the same goals that a group of eight men and thirteen women ascribed to when they gathered together to form the College Graduate Club back in 1896—the precursor organization of the University Club of San Diego which was incorporated in 1909. The primary goal was to bring together people with academic degrees to discuss the important topics of the day. This book provides the historic context in which today's Club operates and offers insight of our members who are leading and interesting San Diegans.

General Manager Matt Parsons. *Photo: Melissa Jacobs—sandiegophoto.com*

A DYNAMIC CLUB

According to the Club's January 2014 newsletter, General Manager Matt Parsons starts a new year by saying, "I am beyond thrilled to share exciting Club updates and goals." He writes, "Goals crafted to enrich your lives by nourishing your mind, body and soul . . . aiming to provide a dynamic foundation that will allow us to deliver on the refined experiences, engaging programs and scholarship objectives that remain the hallmark of your Club." Parsons is referring to his role in the programming phase of the Clubs' recent reinvention.

"This year we are aiming to elevate your lifestyle with great opportunities from some of the newly reinvented committees. Experience travel and

wellness with the Food & Wine Committee, boost your business potential during programs and workshops with the revamped Business Alliance Committee, and build connections on the golf course by joining the newly established Golf Club," said Parsons.

In order to explain why the Club committees are key in the success of the Symphony Towers Club we need to take a step back to the where this dynamic process started, the actual expansion and renovation of this latest Clubhouse. It should be noted that the Symphony Towers Club is the third location and the fourth Clubhouse since its incorporation in 1909. (More about the Clubhouses in Chapters Two and Three.)

GENERAL MANAGERS AT THE SYMPHONY TOWERS CLUB	
Jack Deal	Phillip Gates
Barrett Eifleman	Tommy Trause
Randy Cocke	Matt Parsons
Jim MacDonough	

THE SAN DIEGO UNION-TRIBUNE
C Business
CLASSIFIED ADVERTISING C5
THURSDAY • FEBRUARY 24, 2011

REAL ESTATE + GROWTH

- Dow Jones **–107.01** • 12,105.78
- NASDAQ **–33.43** • 2,722.99
- S&P 500 **–8.04** • 1,307.40
- 10-year Treasury **+0.03** • 3.49%
- Crude Oil **+$4.53** • $98.10
- Gold (N.Y.) **+$12.90** • $1,413.40

Dollar • One U.S. dollar equals:

- Euro **–0.0050** • 0.7274
- Peso **+0.054** • 12.186
- Yen **–0.26** • 82.51

0.9 percent

Monthly increase in construction material costs. Prices have risen 4.9 percent in a year, said the Department of Labor. Biggest increases came in iron and steel — up 4.7 percent for January and up 16.4 percent over 12 months — softwood lumber and steel mill products. "It may be that the inflation people have been predicting for months is finally here," said Anirban Basu, chief economist for Associated Builders and Contractors.

ECONOMY

MARKETS DROP: Stocks fell for a second straight day after clashes in Libya sent oil prices to two-year highs and technology giant Hewlett-Packard said its revenue growth was slowing. Oil companies benefited from higher crude prices, as Chevron was the biggest gainer in the Dow average, rising 1.9 percent, and energy companies in the S&P 500 index rose 2 percent.

MORE BANKS AT RISK: The number of banks at risk of failing rose by 24 to 884 — nearly 12 percent of all federally insured banks — in the fourth quarter, the highest level in 18 years. The largest banks, which account for 1.4 percent of the 7,657 federally insured banks, are driving the bulk of the earnings growth.

FEWER LATE TO WORK: In a change possibly related to layoff worries, 15 percent of workers in a CareerBuilder survey confessed they arrived late to work once a week or more, down from 16 percent in 2009, and 20 percent in 2008. Most-cited reasons: traffic, 30 percent; lack of sleep, 19 percent; and bad weather, 9 percent.

NATION

NEW IPAD ON WAY: Apple is expected to unveil Wednesday the second generation of its successful iPad media tablet, with some speculating that it will have a front-facing camera for video chats, be thinner and lighter or come with a bigger built-in speaker. Also, Apple shareholders rejected a proposal that called for the company to disclose a succession plan for CEO Steve Jobs, who is on an indefinite medical leave for unspecified problems.

ABBOTT DAMAGES OVERTURNED: Abbott Laboratories, maker of arthritis drug Humira, succeeded in a bid to overturn a $1.67 billion patent-infringement verdict won by Johnson & Johnson. The largest patent-related damages award in U.S. history was reversed by the U.S. Court of Appeals for the Federal Circuit in Washington, which ruled that J&J's patent application for competing medicine Remicade never described fully human antibodies.

NEW TAX RULES: Under "income splitting," the IRS is now requiring all same-sex married couples or registered domestic partners in California, Washington state, and Nevada to divide their combined income equally and report it on their separate income tax returns. For some, it will mean more money in their 2010 refund; for others, they'll pay more in taxes.

AUTOS

F-150 RECALL: Under government pressure, Ford Motor said it will recall nearly 150,000 F-150 pickups to fix air bags that could deploy without warning — a fraction of the vehicles the government contends should be called back and repaired. The recall covers trucks from the 2005-2006 model years; owners will be notified and told to bring trucks to dealers.

WHERE DEAL$ ARE MADE

The University Club's recent redesign turned it into even more of a social center. It included renovation of the 1909 Founders' Room (top), a formal-dining area, and the addition of a meeting room (bottom). K.C. ALFRED • U-T PHOTOS

Club's diversifying membership does business with each other, attracts clients in redone space

ROGER SHOWLEY • U-T

The recently redecorated and redesigned University Club is not your great-grandfather's smoke-filled lair.

The 12,500-square-foot private club at the top of the 34-story Symphony Towers downtown still has its Sefton Library, a dark, book-lined inner sanctum where members negotiate deals and sign contracts. (It's named for Thomas W. Sefton, a prominent local banker and philanthropist who died in 2006.)

IN DEPTH C3

Formal dining continues in the "1909 Founders' Room," where coats and ties are mandatory, and a grand piano stands ready to set the mood before symphony concerts.

But now there's a video room with a 105-inch flat-screen TV (and Wii and Xbox connections). Members can check out an iPod if they've left theirs behind.

There are many private clubs in San Diego — yacht clubs, tennis clubs, country clubs, service clubs, a few women's clubs and many garden and hobby clubs.

But none are like the University Club, which began in 1896 as an exclusive alumni club for men and women who graduated from top universities. Now it has no philanthropic or political purpose but serves as a meeting place for members to do business with each other and entertain friends and clients.

"It is really a social center," said general

SEE CLUB • C3

Courtesy of U-T San Diego

THE SAN DIEGO UNION-TRIBUNE | THURSDAY • FEBRUARY 24, 2011 C3

IN DEPTH

The University Club's redesign includes a renovated lounge (top, bottom right). The Laureate Ballroom (bottom left) is used for large events. K.C. ALFRED • U-T PHOTOS

CLUB • Redesign reflects changing tastes, effort to draw 40-somethings

By the numbers

12
Length in feet of the hardwood oak and walnut surfboard/table in the bar built by John Bishop at Hotrod Surfboards

6 to 9
Evening hours when pianist Mike Wofford plays in the dining room

22
The age of the youngest member

100
The age of the oldest member

5,200
Bottle capacity in wine cellar

Fun facts

Mushroom: Soup that's been served more than 20 years without change in recipe, even by current executive chef Eric Mauritzen

Good luck: What members get when they rub the newel post near the front desk; it was salvaged from the 1916 club house.

Board shorts and blazers: Attire for annual "Endless Summer" party.

FROM C1

manager Tommy Trause. "We act as a crossroads for the community. We want to be the place where decisions are made and conversations are had."

Now, with the redesign complete, it's even more of a social hub.

Three 8½-foot "cabanas" have been installed at one end of the Apollo Room, where members and guests can huddle across from each other on two-person couches in tent-like enclosures.

At the other end of the room, which serves as a bar and casual dining space, is a surfboard-shaped table for casual meet-and-greets.

Elsewhere in the club are the 1896 Board Room for videoconferencing; multipurpose Crescendo and Encore rooms; Laureate Ballroom for large events; a wine cellar (where members can store their own cache); and "touchdown rooms" for private conversations by phone, online or with a client.

Doak Belt, 38, said he conducts business over breakfast several times a week at the club. He also participates in the Young Executives Society, which held a beer pong game (a drinking game played with ping-pong balls) before the remodel — something that might have scandalized members of old.

University Club, from grads to dudes

1896: College Graduate Club founded by 21 alumni, including 13 women, primarily from Stanford, UC Berkeley, Harvard and Vassar.

1906: Name changed to University Club, but interest dwindles and it is disbanded the next year.

1908: Men-only University Club founded. Clubhouse rented in 1909 at Fourth Avenue and A Street with accommodations for residents.

1916: Permanent clubhouse built for $29,000 at 1333 Seventh Ave., designed in Spanish style by architect William S. Hebbard.

1970: Replacement clubhouse built for $1 million at same address, designed by architect Frank L. Hope Jr.

1975: Women allowed to join again. Only 12 had done so by 1976.

1989: Club sells building to San Diego Bar Association, is acquired by ClubCorp of America and moves into Symphony Towers.

2010: Club remodeled.

Members under 40 get a break on the dues ($120 instead of $150 per month), but pay the same $1,000 initiation fee. (There are 1,700 members.)

"With the club being redone, there's a lot more space and ways to use the club," said Belt, who lives in La Jolla and works for Innovative Wealth Solutions, a financial planning and tax firm.

The re-established University Club, founded in 1909, had women as members, but over the decades morphed largely into a men's club that appealed to older executives. It was taken over in 1989 by Dallas-based ClubCorp of America and moved to Symphony Towers when that complex was built up and over Copley Symphony Hall.

Sold to KSL Capital Partners in 2006, the company, now called ClubCorp USA, operates 150 clubs throughout the U.S. and has embarked on updating its clubs. San Diego is one of the first to try out some new features.

KSL's resorts division operates La Costa Spa and Resort and owns a piece of the Hotel del Coronado.

Frank Ternasky, an architect with Delawie Bretton Wilkes Rodrigues who oversaw the $2.4 million renovation, said the University Club differs from country clubs, yacht clubs and service clubs.

"This club has no purpose, no goal," he said. "It's purely a business and social club, so the programming is built around its members."

The redesign reflects changing tastes and interests, and the club's efforts to attract 40-somethings to join.

With the casual-dress mode increasingly common in the business world, the redesign made room for an informal dining area near the bar, while retaining the formal dining in the Founders Room.

Women are a growing membership segment — and the two-seat cabana couches were designed primarily for them, Ternasky said.

Pamela Stambaugh, an executive coach, said she and her husband, Larry, joined after moving from Rancho Bernardo to downtown three years ago.

"We didn't have such a facility," in the suburbs, she said.

Her meetings typically took place at a restaurant and coffee shop. "It didn't have the cachet of the University Club — far from it."

She said she now walks to and from the club and sets up meetings in the touchdown rooms.

The club redesign is expected to last 15 or 20 years with a shorter period likely for carpets, table linens and other soft goods.

But some improvements may not prove as necessary as originally thought. For example, the board room has been outfitted with the latest in sound and video conferencing equipment. Ternasky said with the advent of Skype and other computer-conferencing tools, business people don't have as big a need for conference centers.

However, he doesn't say the same for video games.

The doors installed initially to seal off the video game room from the bar are never closed. Members relax with video games in the afternoons, and the games provide a floor show to members who sit nearby.

"We were trying to create a space people enjoy being in, when they can see people in there enjoying themselves," he said.

roger.showley@uniontrib.com
(619) 293-1286
Twitter @rmshowley

THE RENOVATION LEADING TO THE REINVENTION

Leading the renovation team was the former General Manager Tommy Trause. Trause is currently Director of Reinvention and Regional Manager for ClubCorp. According to Trause, "ClubCorp was founded by the late Robert H. Dedman Sr. on November 11, 1957. Fast-forward fifty years and the private club landscape had significantly changed. ClubCorp management knew that the private club industry was in decline and they had an important choice to make: to either find a way to invent what a private club is today or to get out of the private club business. They decided to invent the new private club and hired research consultants from Chicago to interview the Club's membership, to determine their food and beverage preferences, and their activity and lifestyle choices. San Diego, Atlanta, and Orlando were selected as the pilot clubs."

Prior to the physical renovation, Trause and his team spearheaded a concerted effort to bring a broader range of new members including younger executives into the venerable business club. According to Casey Falkner, then the Director of Membership and now ClubCorp's Regional Director of Membership–West Coast City Clubs, "The vision of the 'reinvention' was to build the Club of the future on the foundation and building blocks of the one-hundred-year Club history. In 2009, we spent the year celebrating the centennial and brainstorming what the next generation of a city/business club would include. We looked to the future Club. It was not age-related alone, and significant time was spent on how people do business now and in the future, how members connect. Today, we serve a tremendously diverse membership, in age, industry, interests, and backgrounds—we have found that a

collection of dynamic people is what makes a Club of the future."

In 2010, the stage was set to expand into the entire space of the thirty-fourth floor penthouse. An August 2011 ClubCorp PR release announced a $2.4 million renovation expansion project adding thirty-six-hundred square feet of space and improvements in virtually every area of the Club. At the same time, the Club planned a reinvention that introduced new programming, membership benefits, and services. All construction took place at night and on weekends so as to not interrupt the other building tenants. In all, the expansion project took six months, from June to November 2011, to complete.

"One of the key parts of renovation was member communication," said Trause. "First, we initially heard what our members wanted from their Club.

Casey Falkner and Tommy Trause. *Photo: Margo Schwab/The Social Diary*

"The renovation in San Diego completely rebuilt the Club to make it more accessible to the member on a regular basis. We wanted the club to be an extension of our member's living room and their personality, not just a place for a special event or a power lunch. The Apollo Lounge is a great example of that in the food and beverage price points, the casual attire—it's an easy place for members to use."

—Tommy Trause

Reinvented Apollo Lounge and Bar.

Laureate Ballroom.

Media Room.

1909 Founders Dining Room.

The Crescendo and Encore Rooms.

Touchdown Rooms where members can work away from home and office. All photos on page © *Clay Hayner 2011*

Newsletter *courtesy of ClubCorp Photo. © Clay Hayner 2011*

According to Trause, "Thinking back, the most important benefit was that we created new surroundings that spurred members to use the Club more often, and in doing so, they quickly formed new relationships with other members."

"To sum it up . . . during a brainstorming session Casey Falkner said, 'we are inspired by our heritage and dedicated to our future'. That's the way I feel about the University Club atop Symphony Towers," said Trause.

"The tagline became the mantra in meetings," said Falkner. "And, it was this duality that created the balance of the 'reinvention'."

A NEW ERA

Matt Parsons assumed the helm of the reinvented Club in 2012, with the task of invigorating ongoing membership after the initial excitement of the reinvention ebbed. It was important that his team maintained a balance between the needs of its members with institutional knowledge and the newer members wanting to belong. The most direct way was to expand the Club committees, apply term limits and add a code of conduct.

Then, we kept them abreast of the changes as they happened, tailoring special events such as 'High Heels and Hard Hats', around the move. We offered a weekly construction walkthrough every Friday, and presented a 'Q & A with the Architect'. We added portholes along the construction wall so that members could watch the progress in real time."

But Trause knew that the process of investing in a facility and updating the ambiance does not in itself ensure the success of a private club.

"It was paramount to me that we find new relevance and evolve," said Trause. "We learned quickly that you can't just renovate a Clubhouse, you actually need to reinvent the Club. One is the vehicle for the other. No matter how much you spend on the environment, you have to provide for ways in which members do business. We had to find a way to usher in a new era."

"We are following the continuum forged by Tommy and Casey during the Clubs' reinvention, and bridging renovation and relationship," said Parsons. "We are gathering robust and diverse groups of people to create intelligent programs for all members. Finessing the evolution of the committees may not be easy for some, but we can support a myriad of ideas when members engage in a passionate and caring way. Committee members who feel a sense of ownership about the Club not only link our past to the present, they also ensure our future."

CLUBS WITHIN THE CLUB

Committee logos were designed by Club member Tom Lien, Elevatecreativeinc.com

Food & Wine Committee

The University Club's Food and Wine Committee is dedicated to the advancement of the culinary experience with the introduction of top-tier winemakers and winery owners from throughout the United States and abroad. The Committee consults closely with the Executive Chef, Sommelier, and Director of Food and Beverage to bring innovative and unique programing to the Club's members, while at the same time maintaining a level of culinary excellence. "It's an honor and great pleasure to be tasked with member engagement and satisfaction. I'm really enjoying my tenure in Club leadership," said Beth Binger, Food and Wine Committee Chairperson.

The Food and Wine Committee. Left to right: Justin Stark, Committee Chair Beth Binger, Jason Montoya, Angela Lopez, and Aaron Thun.

Welcome Council

The Welcome Council invites new members and offers an instant connection. The group fosters friendships by participating in many Club events. Front row, left to right: Phyllis Speer, Gwendolyn Taylor-Holmes, Chairperson Rose Avila, and Michelle Langmaid. Back row, left to right: Debra Patterson, Mark Rauch, Art Salindong, Jeana Wallace, Hayden Manning, and Lauren Scobel. *Photo: Julie Walke*

Business Alliance

Business Forward was created in 2014 to provide members with business focused networking opportunities and forums. "We align with our historic tradition in 'promoting art, literature, and general culture," said Co-Chair Michelle Belgar. Pictured clockwise: Co-Chair Justin Frisco, Josh Koehnen, Michelle Belgar, Lynne Feldman, Steve Kozyk, Donald Jasko, Joon Han, Lauren Hong, Leigh-Ann Webster, Keith Arnold, and Laura Bull. *Photo: Justin Stark*

17

Arts Committee

Founding Arts Committee at the Maurice Braun Exhibit. Braun was San Diego's most important painter in the mid-twentieth century. Left to right: Jonathan Tibbitts; Dr. Jim Bowers; Jennifer Braun, Maurice Braun's granddaughter; Julie Walke, Arts Committee Chair; and Aldis Browne. *Gates Photography*

2014 Arts Committee. Left to right: Jennifer Nelson, Arts Chair Julie Walke, Tom Lien, Danielle Zhang, Jonathan Tibbitts, and Jesi Betancourt. Not pictured: Dr. Jim Bowers. *Gates Photography*

Giving Group

The University Club's Giving Group, founded by Bob Alden, connects members and the larger San Diego region by facilitating member involvement in charitable organizations through volunteering, contributions, and awareness. Co-Chairs: Dixie Newman and Scott Tritt. Members: Wendy Gillespie, Sabrina Green, Rod Hatley, Martha Phillips, Joanna Wasmuth, and Lisa Wells.

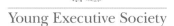

Young Executive Society

YES 2012. Back row, left to right: Jason Montoya, Sean Mayer, David Martin, and Jason Scally. Front row, right to left: Nicole Matthews, Jasmine Corona, Michelle Belgar, and Alexandra Harbushka. *Photo: John Montoya*

In February 2007, *Private Clubs* magazine featured the Young Executive Society. Right to left: Vince Bayard, Michelle Belgar, Justin Frisco, Tisha Carney, David Dawson, Ryan Trenhaile, Misty Moore, Doak Belt, Kassie Eckhart, and Doug Sperber.

Seth O'Byrne, Marybeth Storjohann, Michelle Belgar, Jason Montoya, Jasmin Corona, Sean Mayer, Alexandra Harbushka, and Justin Frisco at the 2012 annual All Aboard event. *Photo by JDixx Photography.*

Executive Women's Council

2004/2005 Executive Women's Council Retreat.

Executive Women's Council 2014 Board. Left to right: Beth O'Dower, Sherry Toby, Dennie Whiteside, Kelly LaRosa, Lisa Wells, Ann Gladys, and Lora Fisher. *Photo: Laura Bull*

Past Presidents of EWC. Left to right: Elizabeth Smith (1998), Jeanne Gahagn (2001), Patricia Wright (1996), Annette Asher (1997), and Janie Davis (2001).

Retired Rear Admiral Ronne Froman, who was Chief of Staff for Mayor Jerry Sanders, spoke to EWC in April 2006. Left to right: Sally Thornton, Sue McNary, and Froman.

Membership Council

The Membership Council invites new members to the Club and offers an instant connection when they join. The group fosters friendships and business connections by participating in many Club events. Christine Baker is the 2014 Chair and has been an amazing supporter of membership. Membership Council and guests enjoyed a recent happy hour.

19

Hiking Club

Golf Committee

The Hiking Club, seen in Balboa Park in 2009, was founded by Jerry Schad (front row, third from right), a veteran outdoorsman, writer, photographer, and author of *Afoot and Afield in San Diego County*, considered to be the bible of San Diego hiking.

The Hiking Club in 2014 at Sunset Cliffs. "Where exercising and socializing include a brief introduction of natural history and cultural information," said Tracey Kennedy, Co-Chair.

The Golf Committee was formed in August 2013 to connect members on and off of the course through outings and events, and caters to golfers of all skill levels. Golf outings take place at ClubCorp Network Courses, Morgan Run Club + Resort, Shadowridge Golf Club, and Omni La Costa Resort & Spa as well as several public courses. Members hold their handicap at the University Club, receive preferred rates, and all receive a personalized golf bag tag. Committee Co-Chairs are Taylor Schulte and Brett Pernicano. Committee members are Erik Brandin, Elizabeth Razanno, Jon Baker, Lisa Goodman, Ben Hunkins, Jen Harris, Joe Beel, Danielle Zhang, and Jimmy Langley.

Left to right: Golf Committee Co-Chairs Brett Pernicano and Taylor Schulte at Shadowridge Golf Club.

On the left is the winning team of four that will be competing at the ClubCorp's 2014 Acura Champions Classic. Pictured (left to right): Pat Phelan, Co-Chair Taylor Schulte, Glen Henderson, Ben Hunkins, Joe Beel, Robin Lipka, Dr. Richard MacDonald, and Charles Hopkins.

Family + Lifestyle Committee

The new Family + Lifestyle Committee. Left to right: Karyn Sklar, Chair Jasmine Corona, Cristiane Valdez, and Helena Koehnen offer family-centric events such as exercise classes and tea parties for the moms/daughters and football games in the media room for the sons/dads. And, date night dinners where childcare is provided. "We want to be a resource for members who are parents that are looking for a way to engage in the Club, but still have family as a priority, said Committee Chair Jasmine Corona.

The Military Network

"The Military Network Club [MNC] generates its own agenda and fosters an environment wherein military and nonmilitary personnel can learn more about one another," said Commander Dan Garcia, U.S. Navy, MNC Co-Chair. Left to right: Bob Alden; Commander Garcia; Ed Langmaid; Commander Joe Darlak, U.S. Navy and MNC Co-Chair; Michelle Langmaid; Ronald Harri; and Colonel Jack Harkins. *Photo: Julie Walke*

Book Club

Started twenty years ago, the Book Club selects from classics and contemporary works and invites local authors to speak. "We engage in a spirited intellectual discussion over a multitude of topics," said Chair Mary Strobbe (right) with EWC Chair Sherry Tobey. http://ucbookclub.blogspot.com *Doug Gates Photography*

Odeon Society

The Odeon Society was born as an intellectual supper club offering Club members an academic discussion over business topics in an intimate setting. Members read a specified article from an esteemed publication, such as *The Harvard Business Review,* ahead of the dinner. "The diversity of opinions is incredibly enlightening," says Chairperson Grace Samodal. "Yes, we all seek personal development, but it is more than that—friendships, business partnerships, and love of good conversation over food."

Chairman Bob McNeeley gives a certificate of appreciation to Grace Samodal for founding the Odeon Society at the Board of Governors meeting October 2013. *Photo by Doug Gates*

21

HIGHLIGHTING THE MILITARY NETWORK

THE UNIVERSITY CLUB ATOP SYMPHONY TOWERS has been a steadfast supporter of the fine men and women of the United States armed forces and values the relationship with each branch of service. The Military Network provides a forum to raise club member awareness of the unique and positive role that the military plays in the San Diego region. This forum, which is social as well as informative, has been well received by many and holds several noteworthy events throughout the year beyond their monthly gatherings. The Military Open House is open to all local military personnel and corresponds with Memorial and Armed Forces Days, allows the University Club and its members to extend their thanks to San Diego military personnel. The University Club hosts a Veterans' Day reception in honor of all who have served in the armed forces of the United States of America; this event has become the de facto venue for the official proclamation that commences Veterans' Week activities in San Diego. During the holidays members of the University Club bring a new gift, for later distribution to children of deployed military personnel by the US Marine Corps' "Toys for Tots" program, in exchange for a hot totty drink provided by the University Club. In 2013 the University Club hosted its inaugural Navy-Army Football Brunch as a fun way to celebrate this time-honored rivalry between the United States Naval and Military Academies.

TOP: Military Network members listen to Colonel Judy Tracy, Army Wounded Warrior Transition Unit, Naval Medical Center San Diego. *Photo: Ed Langmaid 2009*

BOTTOM Admiral Roughhead with Ruby and Larry Maxham.

INSET: Chairman of the Board of Governors Bob McNeely with Chief of Naval Operations Admiral Roughead. *Gates Photography*

FORMATION OF THE BOARD OF GOVERNORS IN 1989

Active committees are important, but equally vital is a solid group of community leaders that offer gravitas and direct connections to some of the city's biggest and most influential businesses and organizations. The first Board of Governors was formed in June 1989 and was generated in part through a purposeful recruitment drive by a small group of anchor tenants.

"Paul Richey from Peat Marwick asked me if I would help him recruit 'bell ringer' founding board members," said Linc Ward, retired head of Pac Bell. "When all was said and done, we acquired about one-third of the founding board."

According to Ward, ClubCorp had to have a game plan for membership and the most strategic move in combining the University Club membership with the ClubCorp name was a good one. "It was brilliant for both, even though, as an outsider, I had nothing to do with that piece of it," said Ward. "I have to give Phil Gildred credit for having a vision in knowing that the University Club was going nowhere in an unimpressive spot."

With regard to the actual formation of the new Board of Governors, Ward felt that

UNIVERSITY CLUB OF SAN DIEGO

FOUNDING BOARD OF GOVERNORS

Phillip L. Gildred, Jr., chairman
Michael Alpert
Richard Atkinson
Robert C. Balink
Vincent Benstead
Steven L. Brezzo
Dirk Broekema, Jr.
Malin Burnham
Harold L. Campbell
J. Dallas Clark
H. Michael Collins
Thomas B. Day
Iven B. Dunphy
Gary H. Estell
Anne Evans
Herbert O. Klein
Kraig Kristofferson
Dan Larsen
Frank H. Laughton
Edgar A. Luce
Karen T. Luce
Donald W. McVay
Michael D. Madigan
Helen Monroe
Bruce Moore
Joseph L. Nemec
William E. Nelson
Kimberlee O'Malley
Oscar Padilla
Joanne M. Pastula
Douglas K. Fay, M.D.
Ralph K. Ferguson
Paul R. Richey
Robert F. Richer
Robert V. Schjel

This brass plate, located in the Club's main hallway, commemorates the first Board of Governors to serve at the Symphony Towers Club in June 1989.

the concept had to be sold to ClubCorp. "The problem is almost fundamental to the structure," said Ward. "The Board of Governors had no real authority over the new Club. Yet you had Phil Gildred and others who were used to having influence and authority. ClubCorp came in, and their people considered this newly formed Board of Governors to be 'in name only'. ClubCorp General Manager Jack Deal was the new kid on the block, and, as can be expected, was not that interested in hearing from our people."

"I was asked to be an advisory member during the move to Symphony Towers because of my personal relationship with Robert and Nancy Dedman," said Dr. James Bowers, philanthropy consultant. "Robert had the right philosophy when he said, 'How many private clubs around the country are struggling to survive?' The private club model should be to run it like a business," said Bowers. "Deal was the right guy for a successful transition. He forged a trust with a close group of advisors to see the project through."

During Deal's tenure, the Symphony Towers Club won the Club of the Year Award. Subsequently, he left to open more Clubs for the company. "He became the new Club impresario," said Bowers. Beyond the obvious growing pains of structure, it took some time for the newly formed Board of Governors to find their relevance in the new club. Its chief resource was to offer valuable connections to San Diego's broader business network.

"The role of the Board of Governors fluctuated

Jack Deal was the first ClubCorp General Manager. The University Club Atop Symphony Towers was named Club of the Year in 1991. *Courtesy of ClubCorp*

LEFT: Linc Ward, founding Board of Governors, President of PacificBell (retired). *Photo: Melissa Jacobs*

RIGHT: Linc Ward and Dr. James Bowers in December 2012. *Gates Photography*

with the general manager changes," said Ward. "However, the Board consistently contributed to membership by bringing in new members and organizations."

For instance, in 1990, Ward brought in the organization called "Military Industry Legal Educational Complex (MILMEC)," founded by Ed Fike, an editor of the *San Diego Union-Tribune*, to have their lunch meetings and annual holiday party at the Club. "MILMEC's objective was to promote flag officers with the community-at-large. Their membership included U.S. Navy Admirals, U.S. Marine Corps Generals, and top business leaders." Twenty-five years later, the organization still continues to have meetings at the Club.

But in the end, the ultimate success of stimulating membership growth is more about the atmosphere and energy of the General Manager and his team rather than simply relying on a Board of Governors.

"In the final analysis the person who took the Club from flat to dynamic is Tommy Trause," adds Ward. "He impacted the membership make-up in many ways which included relaxing the dress code. It had taken two decades for ClubCorp to find a nontypical general manager like Trause. He was able to tap into people's energy, with vision, while relating beautifully with everyone."

BOARD OF GOVERNORS REINVENTED IN 2012

In April 2012, Trause and Dr. Robert McNeely, newly appointed Board Chairman, presided over a reinvented Board of Governors by publishing a new mission. "Our Board is strategic. Our Board shapes, molds, and accelerates the future of San Diego. Not crafted to be a bunch of figureheads—but rather a group of thoughtful, civic and business leaders meeting to collectively craft a better future for the Club and region."[1]

Top and Middle: Tommy Trause addressing the reinvented Board of Governors in April 2012. *All photos Gates Photography*

Bottom: New Chairman Bob McNeely gifts Symphony Towers visionary and longtime Board Chair Doug Wilson with special 1989 vintage to commemorate the year that the University Club became a part of the ClubCorp family and moved into its current home.

Inset: Bob McNeely with Elliot Hirshman.

Left to right: Bob McNeely, Dr. Randy Ward, Jessie Knight, and Chairman Emeritus Douglas Wilson.

Joe Panetta and Dr. Mary Walshok.   Kris Michell and Dr. Randy Ward.   Roxana Foxx and Dr. Mike Reidy.

Left to right: David Bejarano, Jeff Light, and Dan Hom.   Malin Burnham and Chairman Emeritus Wilson.

2014 BOARD OF GOVERNORS

UNIVERSITY CLUB ATOP SYMPHONY TOWERS

BOARD OF GOVERNORS

Robert McNeely—Chairman, Union Bank of California (ret.)
Sherm Harmer—Vice Chair, Urban Housing Partners, Inc.
Nikki Clay—Vice Chair, The Clay Company
Douglas Wilson—Chairman Emeritus, Douglas Wilson Cos.

EXECUTIVE COMMITTEE

James Bowers—Consultant for Philanthropy
Robert Caplan—Seltzer, Caplan, McMahon & Vitek
Reo Carr—*San Diego Business Journal*
Elliot Hirshman—San Diego State University
Jessie Knight—San Diego Gas & Electric
Jeff Light—*San Diego Union-Tribune*
Kris Michell—Downtown San Diego Partnership
Joe Panetta—BIOCOM
Julie Walke—Walke Communications Inc.
Linc Ward—PacBell (retired)
Randy Ward—San Diego County Office of Education

BOARD MEMBERS

David Bejarano—Chief, San Diego Police Dept. (retired)
Beth Binger—Binger Communications, Inc.
Bob Brower—Point Loma Nazarene University
Malin Burnham—Burnham Companies
Alex Butterfield
Constance Carroll—San Diego Community Colleges

Renee Comeau—California Bank & Trust (retired)
James Fitzpatrick—*San Diego Magazine*
Roxana Foxx—Hunter International
Phil Gildred—Gildred Development Cos. (Founding Chair)
Edward Gill—San Diego Symphony
Ben Haddad—California Strategies, LLC
Dan Hom—Focuscom Inc
Joan Jacobs—Qualcomm
Bob Kelly—San Diego Foundation
Jeffrey Lipscomb—AXA Advisors
Robin Madaffer—Schwartz Heidel Sullivan, LLP
Michael McKinnon Jr.—KUSI-TV
Armon Mills—*San Diego Business Journal*
Joanne Pastula—Junior Achievement of San Diego
Jerry Sanders—San Diego Regional Chamber of Commerce
David Schmidt—The Schmidt Group Inc.
Brian Seltzer—Seltzer, Caplan, McMahon & Vitek
Joe Terzi—San Diego Tourism Authority
Thomas Turner—Procopio, Cory Hargreaves & Savitch LLP
Chris Van Gorder—Scripps Health
Luis Vargas—San Diego County District Attorney's Office
Carol Wallace—San Diego Convention Center Corporation
Mary Walshok—University of California San Diego
Yolanda Walther-Meade—ARCS Foundation
Tony Young

"I joined the University Club in 1997 because it was the premier club located downtown for meeting the leaders in the civic and business community," said Robert McNeely, Chairman of the Board of Governors. "In addition to being convenient, I have enjoyed the ambience and outstanding cuisine over the years!" Dr. Robert McNeely who was nominated to the Board of Governors in 2003, and has served on its Executive Committee since 2005.

"The Club has had a profound impact on the fabric of San Diego through the composition of its membership, many of whom are corporate executives, business and community leaders," adds McNeely. "For instance, the Club has indirectly influenced public policy decisions through various programs such as the Distinguished Speakers Program. And our membership, through individual efforts and involvements, has had a significant influence on the positive growth of San Diego."

"It's an honor to serve," said McNeely. "We know that we stand on the shoulders of one of San Diego's oldest institutions and we are proud to promote it locally and globally in our aim to foster solid business and social relationships."

PHILANTHROPY

Contributing back to the community and helping it thrive is critical to the core mission of every dynamic organization. The University Club atop Symphony Towers is no exception. There are several committees involved in philanthropic activities. The "Giving Group" connects members with the non-profit community by hosting events and facilitating volunteerism, contributions, and awareness. The "Young Executive Society" also sets a yearly philanthropic goal. The oldest philanthropic committee at the Symphony Towers Club is the Lamp of Learning Scholarship Committee co-founded by Dr. James Bowers and Linc Ward. Bowers, a forty-year Club member and a twenty-year Governor, serves as Chairman of the Lamp of Learning Scholarship Committee. A former Executive Director of the San Diego Public Library Foundation and Chairman of Scripps Health Foundation, his passion to help those less fortunate inspired him to create this scholarship.

LAMP OF LEARNING SCHOLARSHIP FUND

"I was sitting in an Executive Committee meeting of the Board of Governors in 2004, when I realized that the Club was straying from the original membership intent," said Bowers. "Some of our newer members were not graduates of a university or college—which in the early days of the Club, was a minimum requirement to join."

This statement was true, however Club rules established in 1909 allowed directors to admit up to five people annually without a university education if candidates demonstrated a significant contribution in scientific, professional, or literary pursuits that would equal a college career.[2]

"Obviously the world had changed significantly since the early 1900s," adds Bowers. "But it still seemed to me that we weren't doing enough to contribute academically. So, we reached out to our universities and colleges, welcoming their leaders and educators into our membership. And we sought a meaningful activity for the purpose of creating a Club tradition. We formed a committee to raise five thousand dollars per year for the Lamp of Learning Fund," said Bowers. "We received a unanimous vote of support from the Board of Governors."

"I have to give the credit to Jim," said Ward. "I was his first and early supporter and helped get it started." The committee was comprised of Dr. James Bowers; Linc Ward; Stephen Webber, San Diego State University president; and Jim Dawe, land use attorney. "It became a community asset and meeting ground for diverse people in leadership. We all had a common ground to do good things for education," said Ward.

Co-founder Dr. Jim Bowers with Stephanie Montes and Lamp of Learning Chairman Miguel Montes.

LAMP OF LEARNING SCHOLARS

Dr. Jim Bowers with Joyce Suber, former Regional Director AVID, current Dollars for Scholars Consultant.

Once Club members were behind the program and money was being collected, Bowers reached out into the community to find the right match for a scholarship program beneficiary.

"Someone told me about AVID (Advancement Via Individual Determination)," said Bowers. "It is a college readiness program, supported by the San Diego County Office of Education, which identifies intellectually gifted students throughout our county who need a framework of structured support to reach their full educational potential.[3] I was extremely impressed with Joyce Suber, AVID Regional Director, and knew instantly that we had found the right program." Suber continues to be an active advisor to today's Lamp of Learning Scholarship Committee.

Once AVID was selected, the Club needed a 501(c)(3) organization in which to place the funds. "Club member Bob Kelly, CEO San Diego Foundation, helped us set up the fund," said Bowers. "It became an ideal arrangement for us."

The University Club Atop Symphony Towers members and activities have raised more than $170,000, and funded education for more than forty-five students. The University Club's first scholarship recipient, Jesus Tapia, graduated with a Bachelor's Degree in Mechanical Engineering from UC Berkeley in December 2009. He volunteered as an AVID tutor while working as an after school instructor. He graduated from UC Irvine

AVID—ADVANCEMENT VIA INDIVIDUAL DETERMINATION

AVID, Advancement Via Individual Determination, is a college readiness system for elementary through higher education that is designed to increase schoolwide learning and performance. The AVID College Readiness System (ACRS) accelerates student learning, uses research-based methods of effective instruction, provides meaningful and motivational professional learning, and acts as a catalyst for systemic reform and change.

AVID began in 1980 by Mary Catherine Swanson, then head of the English Department at San Diego's Clairemont High School. The federal courts issued an order to desegregate the city's schools, bringing large numbers of inner city students to suburban schools. While applauding the decision, Swanson wondered how these underserved students would survive at academically acclaimed Clairemont High. Her answer was AVID, an academic elective. But it's more than a program—it's a philosophy: Hold students accountable to the highest standards, provide academic and social support, and they will rise to the challenge.

Beginning with one high school and thirty-two students, AVID now impacts more than seven hundred thousand students in more than forty-nine hundred schools and twenty-eight postsecondary institutions in forty-six states, the District of Columbia, and across sixteen other countries/territories. [Source: www.avid.org]

in December 2012 with a Master's Degree in Aerospace Engineering.

"Jesus is an excellent example of the scholars that we support," said Bowers. "He came to the United States as a young boy who did not speak any English. By the time he was a sophomore at Escondido's Orange Glen High School, he was helping to tutor Spanish-speaking students."

Another scholarship winner, Joey Talia (2009), graduated one year early with a Bachelor of Science Degree in Electrical Engineering and Computer Science, and gave the remainder of his scholarship

back into the Lamp of Learning. He is currently working at Intel Corporation in Silicon Valley.

"I am very proud of my University Club Scholarship," said Talia. "And to have stayed in touch with Dr. Bowers and Julie Walke. It would be my pleasure to come back to San Diego anytime to talk to Club members about my experience with AVID and the Lamp of Learning Scholarship."

"Many of our scholarship recipients are the first person in their family to go to college," adds Bowers. "And the path that some have taken to get to this point just breaks my heart. I wish that we could do more."

2012 Scholarship winners with University Club Judge and Chairman Miguel Montes (left) and committee member Julie Walke (right).

Bowers with 2013 top winner Isreal Barbosa.

The first Lamp of Learning Scholarship winner Jesus Tapia at the California Science Center in Los Angeles in 2013.

Scholarship recipient Joey Talia during a 2013 trip to Machu Pichu.

GIVE BACK: OUR EDUCATIONAL PURPOSE

Raymond Mai, a graduate of Mt. Miguel High, will enroll at UCLA. Mai received the $10,000 University Club Lamp of Learning Scholarship – our highest award.

The University Club's 2011 Lamp of Learning Scholarship Winners

Dr. James Bowers and his Lamp of Learning Scholarship Committee have selected six San Diego area seniors to receive 2011 Lamp of Learning scholarships from the University Club.

Shabazz, Diaz Luevano, Hernandez, Montero-Stabile, and Spieckerman, all received $1,000 University Club awards.

The Lamp of Learning award program, begun in 2004, is funded by tax-deductible contributions from University Club Members, including the 1909 University Club Members. In the past seven years, 38 students – most of them class valedictorians – have won the scholarships and are attending University of California Berkeley, Los Angeles, Riverside, San Diego and Santa Barbara; San Diego State; Cal Poly San Luis Obispo; Princeton; and Stanford.

The six AVID advanced placement students:

Sakeenah Shabazz, a Lincoln High graduate, who placed second in the finals, will attend Georgetown University.

Carolina Diaz Luevano, a graduate of Grossmont High, will attend UCLA.

Diana Hernandez, from Orange Glen High School, will enroll at UC Santa Barbara.

Gabriel Montero-Stabile, a graduate of Montgomery High, will attend California State, Long Beach.

Michael Spieckerman, a graduate of Borrego Springs High, will enroll at Occidental College, Los Angeles.

Support the Lamp of Learning Scholarship

By Sponsoring a New Member!

For the month of July, your Club has committed to contributing half of the New Member Initiation Fees to our scholarship program. Call the Membership Department for more information, to nominate a friend and to support your Club's dedication to education. 619.234.5200

By making a Contribution!

Members are welcome to make contributions to this amazing scholarship program. Simply send to Lamp of Learning Scholarship Foundation, c/o The University Club, 750 B Street, San Diego 92101

The University Club's 2012 Lamp of Learning Scholarship Winners

Dr. James Bowers and his Lamp of Learning Scholarship Committee have selected five San Diego area seniors to receive 2012 Lamp of Learning scholarships from the University Club. Two students, Zelina Gaytan and Eden Aklile, were selected with Highest Distinction. Zelina received the $10,000 Lamp of Learning Scholarship, while Eden was named a Gates Millennium Scholar, the highest award a graduating senior can receive.

The six AVID advanced placement students:

Eden Aklile, a graduate of Serra High School, will be attending UCSD

Zelina Gaytan, a graduate of Mar Vista High School, will be attending UC Berkeley

Seraphina Solders, a graduate of El Capitan High School, will be attending San Diego State University

Marcela Alvarez, a graduate of Montgomery High School, will be attending UCSD

Gustavo Lopez, a graduate of Poway High School, will be attending Cal Poly, San Luis Obispo

The Lamp of Learning award program is funded by tax-deductible contributions from University Club Members, including the 1909 University Club Members. In the past seven years, 43 students – most of them class valedictorians – have won the scholarships and are attending University of California Berkeley, Los Angeles, San Diego and Santa Barbara; San Diego State; Cal Poly San Luis Obispo; Princeton; and Stanford.

31

LAMP OF LEARNING SCHOLARSHIP COMMITTEE TODAY

Dr. Bowers is now Past Chairman. Miguel Montes is Chairman. Committee members are: Paul Bergman, Simon Cottriall, Mary Lou Green, Lori Eisenberg, Liz Laughlin, Steffenie Montes, and Matt Parsons.

According to Bowers, "each year more than three hundred high school juniors apply." A team of AVID counselors reviews the applications and selects up to fifteen students for the Lamp of Learning Committee to interview. The committee selects five or six of students to be semifinalists through their junior year. The following May, when the semifinalists are high school seniors, the committee interviews them a second time to determine who will win the $10,000 scholarship with the other semifinalists receiving $2,000 each.

The 1909 University Club of San Diego Board of Directors considers the Lamp of Learning Scholarship to be of upmost importance and has supported the program for many years. In 2009, they donated a one-time gift of $10,000 to commemorate the Centennial Anniversary. That year, two scholars received a $10,000 prize. Members of the Board have also volunteered in the scholarship interview process. "As the historic entity of the University Club," said Julie Walke, 1909 Board President, "one of our main responsibilities is to promote higher education. The Lamp of Learning Scholarship Fund is a worthy cause and we are proud to play a part." (More about the 1909 Board of Directors later in this chapter and also in Chapter 3.)

Throughout each year, ClubCorp staff inspire members to generate donations to the Lamp of Learning Scholarship through special membership incentives and major fundraising events, such as Suit & Tie and 'Tis the Season.

According to Matt Parsons, "We support the Lamp of Learning Scholarship because it is one of the most rewarding efforts that the Club puts forth in supporting some of San Diego's best and brightest students."

"It has been a true pleasure to participate on the Lamp of Learning Committee," said Parsons. "These young scholars have endured and overcome incredible personal hardships to excel in their classes, and maybe more importantly, make a dramatic contribution within their communities. They inspire all of us to be our best. And, give hope that bright young minds will contribute to a better tomorrow."

LAMP OF LEARNING $10,000 SCHOLARSHIP WINNERS

2005—Jesus Tapia, UC Berkeley
2006—Mana Hagos, UCLA
2007—Adrian Lopez, UCSD
2008—Esmeralda Tovar, UCLA
2009—Joey Talia, UC Berkeley
2010 – Christian Vigil, UC Berkeley
2010—Masiha Noori, UCSD
2011—Raymond Mai, UCLA
2012—Zelina Gaytan, USD
2013—Israel Barbosa, UCSD
2014—Lauren Fleming, UC Irvine

FUNDRAISING EVENT TO BENEFIT THE LAMP OF LEARNING FUND

Black Tie and Blue Jeans—now called Suit & Tie is an annual event to benefit the Lamp of Learning Scholarship Fund among other charities.
Photos © Gates Photography

Bob and Dolores McNeely.

Jerry Schad with Peg Reiter.

Alexander Butterfield and Audrey Geisel.

33

Mary Lou and Terry Green.

Kevin and Tracey Kennedy.

THE LEGACY BOARD: THE 1909 UNIVERSITY CLUB OF SAN DIEGO, INC.

The origins of the University Club of San Diego started in 1896 with the College Graduate Club and a meeting of twenty-one individuals (eight men and thirteen women), who gathered together people with academic degrees to discuss the current topics of the day.[4] This group suffered a decline in its original strength and enthusiasm, so in May 1906 the group changed its name to the University Club hoping to attract new members. However, even with the new Club name and amended rules, apparent member disinterest caused the termination of the activities in 1907.[5] Later that year, some of the male University Club members started meeting with a group who belonged to college fraternities to form an inter-fraternity, male-only organization in 1908. They met on December 8, 1908, to formally organize the club that was incorporated in 1909 with Russell C. Allen, a former member of the College Graduate Club, elected as the first President.

This organization continues to operate as one of San Diego's oldest corporations, having survived four Clubhouses in three locations, and a metamorphous to its current existence, as a philanthropic Board of Directors.

In 1989, after the move to Symphony Towers, the University Club could have ceased to exist. However, a handful of leaders thought it prudent not to dissolve the corporate entity but maintain its presence in tandem with ClubCorp. The rationale was not to compete in the private club business but rather to prevent the possible loss of a historic organization should Dallas-based ClubCorp decide, for whatever reason, to cease doing business in San Diego. The Joinder Agreement between the parties, sought an equitable arrangement by which the original corporation was renamed the 1909 University

Club of San Diego, Inc., and that it would lease the University Club name to ClubCorp but retain ownership of the University Club logo. The new ClubCorp entity was named the University Club Atop Symphony Towers. The agreement also outlined that the 1909 Club Board of Directors would exhibit their collection of fine art paintings, books, and historic artifacts at the Symphony Towers Club, while promising to maintain the collection.

The 1909 Board of Directors has not easily been understood by most of the ClubCorp General Managers, not knowing how to effectively tap into the Board's assets and resources in support of the new Club. To be fair, the 1909 Board of Directors also took many years to evolve into its

1909 UNIVERSITY CLUB OF SAN DIEGO, INC. BOARD OF DIRECTORS

Front row, left to right: Julie Walke, President; Rob Scott, Secretary; and Ann Beard, Board Member. Back row, left to right: Mike Bixler, Board Member; Suzanne Swift, Vice President; Don Fine, Chief Financial Officer, and James Alcorn, Board Member. Not pictured: Phil Gildred, Board Member Emeritus. *Photo: Melissa Jacobs*

current activity level. Today, the 1909 Board sponsors and promotes the activities and programs of the Symphony Towers Club. They have been diligently and quietly protecting a small, but noteworthy collection of fine art and artifacts; making annual donations to the Lamp of Learning Scholarship Fund; contracting with arts institutions and insuring the artwork for the Arts Committee exhibitions; and maintaining the history of the University Club of San Diego.

"It was Tommy Trause who plugged into our shared value and significance," said Julie Walke, President, 1909 University Club of San Diego, Inc. "Together, we came up with the idea of forming the Arts Committee as both of us realized that quarterly art installations couldn't be successfully executed without the legal and financial support of the 1909 Board. The 1909 Board, on the other hand was in pursuit for a way to be relevant in the modern Club."

The 1909 University Club Board gave $10,000 in honor of it's One-hundredth Anniversary. Vice President Suzanne Swift and President Julie Walke present the check to Lamp of Learning Scholarship Chairman Dr. James Bowers and General Manager Tommy Trause.

MEMBER ACTIVITIES

DISTINGUISHED SPEAKER EVENTS

The Distinguished Speaker Series, founded by David Schmidt in 2001 as a return to the original speaker forum from the early 1900s. It is a monthly breakfast event whereby newsmakers from San Diego and beyond keep members current on politics, media, arts, and business. *Photos © Gates Photography*

Left to right: Masha Sewell, Trudy Stambook, Jim Silverwood, and Robert Watkins.

Lauren and Haney Hong and Larry Maxham.

Left to right: David Schmidt, Carl DeMaio, Jerry Sanders, and John Dadian.

San Diego Update in the Media Breakfast. Left to right: Jeff Light, Reo Carr, Jeff Powers, Jim Laslavic, Erin Meanley, and Beth Binger.

Carmen Vann.

Left to right: Kathleen Haidl, Marty Weinstein, Sahs Favelukis, and Peter Barnes.

Nasir Pasha and A. J. Alluin.

ART EVENTS

Robin Lipman and Andrea Muir at the Burkhart Opening.

Left to right: Anne Hoiberg, Ashley Gardner, and guest.

The 1909 Board of Directors is the sponsoring organization supporting the ongoing art exhibits dedicated to San Diego's finest art institutions, museums, and collections by offering members a glimpse of some of the best art of California. © Doug Gates Photography

Left to right: Salah Hassanein, Erika Tori, Zandra Rhodes, Maria Munroe Browne, and Aldis Browne.

Hans Burkhardt Exhibit in honor of the San Diego Museum of Art.

Costume and set designs from *Aida* by Zandra Rhodes in honor of the San Diego Opera in association with the La Jolla Athenaeum.

Do Ho Suh sculpture which is a part of the Stuart Collection, UCSD.

Carlette Lewis and Jacqueline Hawkins.

ClubCorp ECO Eric Affeldt is such a big fan of Zandra Rhodes designs that he purchased three pieces. Affeldt is pictured here with Rhodes and Julie Walke at ClubCorp Inc. headquarters in Dallas. *Photo courtesy of ClubCorp*

Left to right: Russell King, Zandra Rhodes, and Joseph Anthony.

d'Arcy Miller, Matt Parsons, and guest at the Burkhardt Opening.

"Context and Choreography: The Archtecture of Rob Wellington Quigley" (right) in honor of the opening of the San Diego Central Library with longtime Club member James Dawe.

Left to right: Nikki Klugh, Tracy Massimo, and Ana Yufe.

Lauren Hong, Stefan Kramer, Danielle Zhang, Caio Buzzonlini, and Grace Samodal at the Quigley Opening.

The Woven World from the Mingei Museum.
© Gates Photography

Left to right: Paul Bergman, Sandra Bergman, and Jerry Strayver.

Left to right: Wendy Gillespie; Shirley Fishman, La Jolla Playhouse Dramaturg; and Lynelle Lynch, La Jolla Playhouse Board Chair.

Tribute to Phenomenal Exhibit. © Gates Photography

Rob Scott reviews a tribute to the La Jolla Playhouse.

41

YOUNG EXECUTIVE SOCIETY (YES) ANNUAL ALL ABOARD EVENT

Photos © J Dixx

CHEESE AND CRAFT BEER PAIRING EVENT

Favorite members events usually feature fine food, handmade cocktails, good wine, and craft beer. Just like the House of Castello Cheese and Craft Beer Pairing event. *Photos © Gates Photography*

THE UNIVERSITY CLUB ATOP SYMPHONY TOWERS TEAM

"The University Club Employee Partners are a critical component to providing exceptional service to the members. At the Symphony Towers Club we have been fortunate to have retained fifteen employee partners for five years or more, and six of them for over twenty years. We see this a part of the Club's heritage in that they bring forth some of the traditions from the past while supporting our members of today. The continued growth and success of the University Club is in large part due to the exceptional work that is done every day by the employee partners. They are considered to be the finest serving the finest." —Matt Parsons, General Manager

Management Team with Eric Affeldt, President and CEO, ClubCorp, in January 2014. Left to right: Laura Bull, Kayla Craig, Brigette Bower, Casey Falkner, Eric Affeldt, Matt Parsons, Lauren Scobel, Diane Fortakoff, and Ed Nesfield. *Gates Photography*

Member Relations Director Lauren Scobel with the Member Services Team. Left to right: Lauren Scobel, Kat Bacud, Deanna Cuadras, Danielle Burciaga, and Robbie Chappelle. *Photo: Julie Walke*

Wine Sommelier Aaron Thun. *Photo: Laura Bull*

Jose Guzman first started working for the University Club in the early 1980s and he still works at the Club today. "I love working in a club atmosphere. The members treat me kindly and they have become more like family members rather than customers. I want to be a part of this membership for the rest of my working life," said Guzman.

Food and Beverage Team. Left to right: Jose Dominguez, Director of Operations Justin Stark, Executive Chef Brad Hightow, Sam Southwick, Lee Dunteman, and A. J. Graybill. *Photo: Julie Walke*

First-rate service and first-rate staff. © *Clay Hayner 2011*

Staff being photographed at the Charity Classic Event in 2013. *Photo by Doug Gates*

Membership Directors Amy Mitchell and Mike Iaco. *Photo: Julie Walke*

Matthew and Casey Falkner.

Kayla Craig, Danielle Burciaga, and Deanna Cuadras get ready for Suit & Tie 2013.

ENDNOTES

1. Trause, Board of Governors Reinvented presentation. ClubCorp, April 13, 2012.

2. "Terrace Leased As University Club House," *San Diego Union*, June 6, 1990, p. 16.

3. Region IX What is AVID?, San Diego County Office of Education, 2011–2012.

4. See *The University Club of San Diego, Membership Roster*, 1980–81.

5. Sylvia K. Flanigan, "Social and Intellectual Affiliation: Formation and Growth of San Diego's University Club," *Journal of San Diego History*, Winter 1985, pp. 46–47.

MERRILL

CHAPTER TWO

BUILD IT AND THEY WILL COME

The City of San Diego today is the second largest city in California, however it was a growing metropolis in the 1970s that ran a distant third to Los Angeles and San Francisco. City leadership knew that they needed to revitalize the central core and to try to capitalize on the deep-water port, as businesses had left downtown for the suburbs. The vitality of downtown's nightlife was suffering, especially south of Market Street, as the town still held the remnants of the seedier side of seagoing life.

In 1972, the City Council approved an urban design plan that eventually encompassed fifteen blocks. What began as a city improvement project to refurbish San Diego's historic town plaza mushroomed into one of the major downtown redevelopment plans of the 1970s and 1980s.[1] Although

not the only shopping district, San Diego's urban renaissance got a jumpstart in August 1985, when the multilevel shopping center named after Alonso Horton—the nineteenth century real estate developer who put San Diego on the map—opened in the Gaslamp Quarter. Horton Plaza's innovative design, appealing bright colors, and massive parking structure brought suburbanites in droves to shop and dine downtown for the first time in decades.

The Gaslamp Quarter may have spurred the growth, but it was not the only downtown area being redeveloped. Civic visionaries led the 1986 construction expansion of a city block between A and B Streets and bounded by Seventh and Eighth Avenues. Already developed by the Gildred family was the well-known Fox Theater. Built in 1929, the Gothic-revival luxury movie theater had over time become home to the San Diego Symphony. Architects envisioned that the new high rise, soon to be called Symphony Towers, would be constructed around the existing theater. Once built, Symphony Towers would be the tallest building in San Diego at 499 feet. Until two years later when One American Plaza was built to a height of 500 feet. The Symphony Towers Building may be the second tallest building in San Diego today, but the spectacular views from the University Club Atop Symphony Towers outtop them all.

San Diego skyline 1989. *Courtesy of Douglas Wilson Companies*

Douglas Wilson (right) and Phil Gildred Jr. were the two people at the center of the Symphony Towers Project. Gildred, whose family had built the legendary Fox Theater was past President at the University Club. The thirty-three-year-old Wilson brought youthful enthusiasm and a new vision as Executive Vice-president of Charlton-Raynd Development Company for Symphony Towers. *Photo by Melissa Jacobs*

A CLUB WITH A HISTORY

Across the street from Symphony Towers development stood the Clubhouse of the then-sixty-five-year-old privately held, member-owned University Club of San Diego. The first Clubhouse was a mansion on the northwest corner of Fourth Avenue and A Street. The Club moved to Seventh Avenue and A Street in 1916, and constructed a four-story headquarters designed by noted architect William S. Hebbard, the 1911 University Club President. The second Clubhouse was completed and furnished for $33,500.

PHIL GILDRED JR.

"In 1927 my father purchased this entire block and proceeded to build the Fox Theater and garage and a four-story Montgomery Ward department store. Construction was completed in 1929. In the late 1950s Montgomery Ward vacated the department store.

"In the early 1960s my brother and I embarked on a remodel program to convert the department store space into office space. This was a successful undertaking all the way through the 1980s when we sold the building.

"In the mid-1980s Doug Wilson and his associates purchased the building and proceeded with the planning of a multiuse project to include a hotel tower, garage, and high-rise office tower with the University Club occupying the top floor, all covering the theater now known as Symphony Hall.

"The entire project has been a huge success and the Gildred family is very proud of the final outcome."

THE HISTORY OF THE FOX THEATER (Now Symphony Hall)

ON OCTOBER 29, 1929, THE STOCK MARKET CRASHED, launching American into the Great Depression. Ten days later, on November 8, the Fox Theater opening was celebrated by between 30,000 and 100,000 of the city's 145,000-plus residents. The party started at 7:30 p.m. with a parade from lower Broadway to the spotlight-swept theater. Thousands of San Diegans lined the parade route—treated to a free streetcar transportation courtesy of the theater chain—cheered a police motorcycle escort, American Legion Band, myriad floats, limousines bearing the "Fox Fiesta Girls," and autos with Hollywood celebrities. The parade ended at a four-block area surrounding the theater cordoned off for reviewing stand introductions of Will Rogers, Buster Keaton, Marie Dresser, and Jackie Coogan. Also in attendance were stars such as George Jessell, Billie Dove, Joe E. Brown, Victor McLaglen, George O'Brian, Anita Page, and "Buddy" Rogers. All followed by a fireworks display. Once inside, the show began with a Fox Movietone newsreel, followed by a *Silly Symphony* cartoon. Live entertainment preceded the movie, with a brother-and-sister team Franchon and Marco presented "Jazz Temple," a stage show with the Fox Symphony Orchestra led by local favorite Al Lyon, followed by eight high-kicking chorus girls called the Franchonettes. The main event was the movie *They Had to See Paris*, the first "talkie," starring humorist Will Rogers. All three thousand opening night tickets were sold out at cost of $5 apiece.

LEFT: Fox Theater Grand Opening in November 1929. *Courtesy of Gildred Companies*

TOP RIGHT: Fox Theater interior, 1929. *Courtesy of Gildred Companies*

BOTTOM RIGHT: George Gildred Jr. and Alison Gildred (right) photographed at the Alfred Mitchell art opening with Sally Bixler in 2013. *Gates Photography*

Downtown aerial circa 1930s: Notice the airplane east of the El Cortez that is flying toward Lindberg Field, San Diego. *Courtesy of Gildred Companies*

In 1969, the second Clubhouse was razed, and, at a cost of $1 million, the current larger three-story building was erected on property spanning the same lot as well as on a piece of land on the adjacent corner that the Club had purchased.[2]

"In the late sixties it became very apparent that our aging Clubhouse did not provide adequate space for the membership and was in need of many major repairs," said Philip Gildred, 1983 University Club President. "The Clubhouse really needed to be replaced. With the help of the City Building Department threatening to condemn the building, it was finally decided to raze the old Clubhouse and construct a new one. We covered the old parking lot, adding an additional five thousand square feet that enlarged the Clubhouse footprint to ten thousand square feet."

According to Gildred, "In order to make the new building a reality, a fundraising program was set in place. It was decided that it would be much easier and palatable to raise the needed funds if we issued debentures rather than asking for an outright gift. This fundraising program was successful enough for the Club to eventually close the existing location and move to the top floor of the recently completed Home Tower Building on Seventh and Broadway during construction. While there, fundraising continued until the final debentures were sold." The new building design included a men's fitness facility, a bar with a fireplace, a main dining room, small dining room, library, card room, free underground parking, and valet parking.

During the late 1970s, the University Club experienced lackluster membership, as did the three other private member clubs in the city (the Cuyamaca

Club, the San Diego Athletic Club in the Harcourt Brace Building, and the Tambo de Oro Club in the Union Bank Building). Perhaps this situation reflected the changing societal norms that started in the 1960s or the business shift away from downtown in 1980s toward the Golden Triangle area with its proximity to La Jolla and the burgeoning campus of University of California San Diego.

Had the heyday of San Diego's private social and business clubs come and gone? It depended on with whom you spoke—those who knew the fiscal reality of running a member-owned club versus those who felt nostalgic over its long and storied past. Either way, leaders of the University Club were anxious to find ways to ensure the future of the Club.

In 1973, Club leaders toyed with the idea of merging with the Cuyamaca Club, California's oldest private club. Fortuitously backed by banker and industrialist C. Arnholt Smith, the Cuyamaca Club had moved into the elegantly appointed Westgate Executive House in 1971—a Clubhouse that

The second Clubhouse. In 1907, William S. Hebbard, along with Edgar A. Luce and Frank von Tesmar, reorganized the floundering University Club of San Diego. They changed it to an organization to which all male college alumni were eligible. In 1909, the University Club was formally incorporated as a bona fide organization with Hebbard, Luce, E. L. Hardy, Julius Wangenheim, and D. D. Whedon writing the rules and by-laws. In 1911, Hebbard assumed the presidency of this organization. © San Diego History Center

boasted opulent décor, overnight accommodations, spa and fitness facilities, and affiliation with a fifty-six clubs worldwide.

According to Sally Bullard Thornton, who wrote an article about the Cuyamaca Club for the *Journal of San Diego History*, "Within less than two years [1973] there were negotiations with the University Club to include their 650 members with the Cuyamaca Club's 1,200 members. But after three weeks, the University Club decided to retain their autonomy and discontinued the talks."[3] The Cuyamaca Club finally closed its doors in 1987 after C. Arnholt Smith was convicted of embezzlement of $8.9 million and for tax fraud.

The University Club leaders must have felt that they dodged a bullet after they pulled out of the Cuyamaca deal because the Club's history and good reputation remained intact.

In 1970, the second Clubhouse to be developed on Seventh Avenue was an expanded footprint that included the property adjacent to A Street. Photo circa 1981. © San Diego History Center

THE ROUND TABLE

For many years and with fond reminiscence there was a University Club tradition that is considered to have been at the center of the fabric of the Club. It was the large fifteen-foot diameter "Round Table" located in the center of the main dining room in the second Clubhouse.

According to Philip Gildred, "It all ties in with the Club." He was a young member who had just joined the Club in 1961. "Our offices were in the Fox Building at Seventh and A Street and the Club was a convenient place to have lunch. I was working in the family business for my father Phillip Gildred Sr. In those days, the Fox Building was a fifty-thousand-square-foot space that housed Montgomery Ward, which had moved to Mission Valley in the late 1950s, offices, and parking. It was my job to find a tenant but no one wanted to move downtown. I was wondering whether we should remodel the space into offices. I met with an architect but was disappointed at our apparent options. A couple of weeks later, I sat at the Round Table and met Leonard Teyssier. I told him that we thought we should remodel but that, according to the architect, we cannot use brick. Leonard told me 'it was the craziest thing that he had ever heard in his life'. As an outcome of that lunch at the Round Table, we met the following week, I was flabbergasted at the drawings he had and he turned into our contractor—the Fox Building was torn down except for the theater."

UNESCORTED WOMEN WERE NEVER SEATED AT THE ROUND TABLE

"Some habits are hard to break," said Mike Bixler, President 1985–1986. "I will never forget the time when I was seated at the Round Table when the maître d came up to me with an odd look on his face. He whispered, 'I need your assistance, there is a young lady who is unescorted, who wants to come into the main dining room and be seated at the Round Table. I told her that this request was unusual.'"

Not wanting to be argumentative Bixler explained that it was tradition that women were to be escorted when dining at the Round Table. She asked, "what will happen if I sit down?" To which Bixler replied, "probably nothing and they will be polite. But if they see you dining at the Round Table frequently, they may not come again and I would hate to ruffle the feathers of the older men." Bixler was concerned that they may act differently while women were present. Or worse, choose to go to the Grant Grill instead eating lunch at the Club. And, the Club needed the lunch business. "If I recall, she ate at the table but chose not to do so on a regular basis," said Bixler."But this is an example of the ways that Club members needed to modernize their thinking after we voted to attract female members."

The University Club of the early 1970s was a very different place from the one we know today. Most noticeably, the Club was only open to men, even though several women were integral to the Club's early formation in 1896.

Women were voted into the Club as members in April 1975. Karen Johnson, a retired school principal from St. Paul, Minnesota, became the first woman member. By October of that year, the Club had three woman members.[4]

Prior to 1975, ladies were invited as guests but they were not allowed to dine at the coveted *round table* that sat in the center of the main dining room. Much discussion took place over how to accommodate the ladies. Member Edgar Luce, 1945 University Club President, offered to pay to furnish in a small dining room adjacent to the main dining room. From that moment forth the room was mockingly referred to as the *Luce women's dining room.*

According to the *San Diego Union-Tribune*'s Roger Showley, when women were invited to join, it was "a step reportedly taken to help pay for the new $1-million Clubhouse at Seventh Avenue and A Street. By 1985, the initiation fee was $300 and the monthly dues were $60."[5]

HISTORY OF THE ROUND TABLE

THE UNIVERSITY CLUB NEWSLETTER IN JULY 1987 featured a story about the Round Table, which had been newly refurbished. According to Club member Len Storay (Club President 1963), "The Round Table was originally known as the 'Long Table' and was the main piece of furniture in the main dining room in the old Clubhouse (1916–1970). It was also the only piece of furniture saved from the old Clubhouse. Some of the regulars who used to frequent the Round Table were Vice Admiral William 'Bill' Munroe; Gordon McNary, Vice President of San Diego Trust & Savings Bank; Peter Bullard; Fred Conrad, Club President 1965; Howard Levinson, Club President 1975; Steve Oggel, Club President 1980; Bill Hiscock, Club President 1984; and Mike Bixler, Club President 1985 and 1986; just to name a few."

ABOVE: Club members dine around the refinished Round Table.

RIGHT: The new Symphony Towers Club surfboard-shaped table located in the Apollo Lounge is a modern-day nod to the Round Table tradition from the old Clubhouses. © *Clay Hayner 2011*

After a decade of slow membership growth and increased expenses, loyal members and community leaders such as Thomas W. Sefton and his San Diego Trust & Savings Bank stepped in to bolster the Club's finances. Sefton encouraged other members, such as the Crabtree and Scripps families to also contribute, but everyone knew that this was only a stopgap measure. So, the stage was set when the development of the Fox Theater block came under discussion.

A NEW CLUB ON THE HORIZON

"We were wrapping up a Board meeting when attorney William "Bill" Hiscock, 1984 University Club President, suggested that we have a glass of wine afterwards," said Gildred. "He started talking about the new Symphony Towers development and had heard that there was intention to put a nice dining club at the top of the building. Hiscock suggested that I meet with the developer."

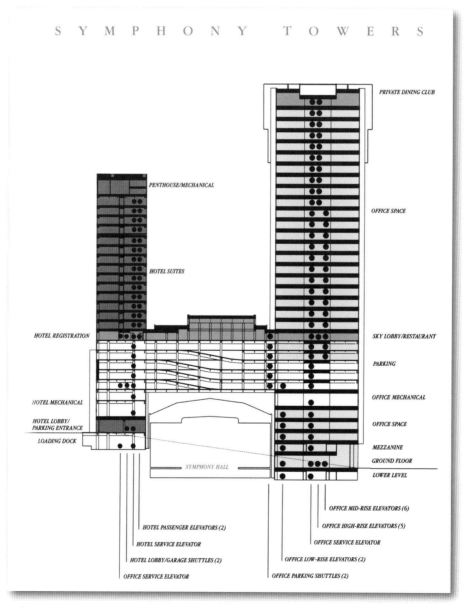

S Y M P H O N Y   T O W E R S

PRIVATE DINING CLUB

OFFICE SPACE

PENTHOUSE/MECHANICAL

HOTEL SUITES

HOTEL REGISTRATION

SKY LOBBY/RESTAURANT

PARKING

OFFICE MECHANICAL

HOTEL MECHANICAL

OFFICE SPACE

HOTEL LOBBY/
PARKING ENTRANCE

MEZZANINE

LOADING DOCK

GROUND FLOOR

SYMPHONY HALL

LOWER LEVEL

OFFICE MID-RISE ELEVATORS (6)

HOTEL PASSENGER ELEVATORS (2)

OFFICE HIGH-RISE ELEVATORS (5)

HOTEL SERVICE ELEVATOR

OFFICE SERVICE ELEVATOR

HOTEL LOBBY/GARAGE SHUTTLES (2)

OFFICE LOW-RISE ELEVATORS (2)

OFFICE SERVICE ELEVATOR

OFFICE PARKING SHUTTLES (2)

Architectural section of Symphony Towers Project. *Courtesy of Douglas Wilson Companies*

Membership Office
1301 7th Avenue
San Diego, California 92101
(619) 234-5200

February 1989

The University Club
atop Symphony Towers

Progress Report

WELCOME TO THE
UNIVERSITY
CLUB

'Let the Construction Begin!"
(l. to r.) Doug Wilson, Executive
Vice President of Charlton-Raynd
Development Co.; Philip L.
Gildred, Jr., Chairman of the
Founding Board of Governors;
and Dan Larsen, Board Member
cut the ribbon to signify
commencement of work to
complete the interior finishes of
the Club.

CONSTRUCTION UNDERWAY

T here is no silence atop Symphony Towers.

The hum of saws, rhythm of beating hammers and vibrations from power drills assure Members and invitees alike that the University Club is indeed taking shape.

Director of Construction, Herb Goodman, reports that construction on the thirty-fourth floor of Symphony Towers is progressing rapidly. New duct work suitable for the Club is now being fabricated so that it can be installed soon, along with the electricity and plumbing. The kitchen will be installed in March and training of the Club's staff will begin soon thereafter.

"Final selection of the Club's general contractor for interior finishes took place in late January. Hallenbeck, Chamorro & Associates is providing the construction documents. We have been very pleased with their efforts and cooperation to date," reports Goodman.

The Club is scheduled to open in early spring. That's when all the loud hammering will cease and the soft music will begin.

SEFTON
LIBRARY

Thomas W. Sefton (left) and Doug Wilson (right).

After that meeting, University Club President Philip Gildred Jr., walked over to the Imperial Bank Building, entered the suite of Charlton Rand Ventures and introduced himself to Douglas Wilson.

"I told the secretary who I was," said Gildred. "Douglas Wilson responded saying he absolutely wanted to meet me." Wilson, a Denver transplant, would become a new Club member in order to see the deal through.

According to Gildred, "During that first meeting, we talked about an 'instant club' concept. A Club which had lots of civic leaders and old San Diegans such as the membership of the University Club. The idea was not to build a restaurant for the masses."

"Phil said, 'what if we could figure out a way to take our existing membership of six hundred people and make them the nucleus of the new club.' On the face of it, it seemed like a good idea. But I was young

BY THE NUMBERS

✦ The Symphony Towers project cost $143.5 million and was developed by managing partner London & Edinburgh Trust and Charlton Rand.

✦ Over 7,300 pieces of sunset red and carnelian granite were used at a weight of 2,085,255 pounds (approximately).

✦ About four miles of electrical pipe and twenty miles of wire run through the project.

✦ The five high-rise elevators travel from ground level to the penthouse at one thousand feet per minute.

and there were some old-timers who were trying to do backroom deals to derail the idea," said Wilson.

Gildred reported back to the Board of Directors with mixed results. "There were a lot of guys who didn't want it. But then Ann Parode, who was Senior Vice President and legal counsel for San Diego Trust & Savings Bank, said 'this sounds really good and I think that we should move forward'. Parode's opinion was highly regarded as a direct advisor to San Diego Trust President Tom Sefton. I wasn't about to disagree with Tom," said Gildred.

The possible move raised an issue that divided members and caused hard feelings. "Back in the day when we were issuing the building debentures, we never 'sold' the idea to our members that this was a good investment scheme," said Philip Gildred. "I always felt that they [members] should hold onto them. It was the right thing to do."

"It must be pointed out that the success of reaching our goal by selling the debentures was not because the debentures were a good investment," adds Gildred. "The successful selling of the debentures

was due to the fact that the members that participated loved the Club and wanted it to succeed. Once we were planning to sell the Clubhouse and move to Symphony Towers, some of the members wanted money for their debentures while other thought that was a selfish position because we had all liked and used the Club's facilities for decades."

Wilson and Gildred may have been the two people at the center of the project because the Gildred Company had built the legendary Fox Theater, while the thirty-three-year-old Wilson brought youthful enthusiasm and vision for a new San Diego, but as most big projects go, it takes other leaders to shift opinions and make sure that others follow the vision. Mike Bixler, who tactfully worked behind-the-scenes in support of fiscal solvency, executed that role.

The goal of the development team was to introduce the Private Club concept for the top floor of the new Symphony Towers Building. The lease was to be negotiated by Luce Forward and introduce us to a private club management company called ClubCorp, headquartered in Dallas.

"Beyond the debentures issue, the only other deep membership divide was over the Symphony Towers Building," said Mike Bixler, 1985 and 1986 University Club President. "It was a division between those who were totally ensconced with the idea of a privately owned club with free parking, an athletic facility, a card room, and a small, intimate lounge; versus the allure of going across the street for first-rate dining and professional club management. It was absolutely fair to say that there was substantial controversy in the membership over the answer of this question."

A majority of the Board of Directors saw the move to Symphony Towers as a catalyst for change. The

University Club had older and less socially active members; finances had always been a struggle; and a twenty-five-year-old facility that had not been fully maintained. The sky-high 360-degree view and $1-million investment in décor were all powerful draws. "The bonus was to escape the obligation of managing a club," adds Bixler.

"As past-President in 1986, when the project was first introduced, I had been involved every step of the way," adds Bixler. "I saw my role as that of a diplomat; to ensure that there was full and fair discussion."

Adding another layer of complexity to the move was an alternative development idea introduced by Barry Newman, 1987 University Club President. This competing development was floated to the Board of Directors and then to the membership at large. Tentatively called the Financial Gateway project, developer Trammell Crow Company provided floor plans for a 17,589-square-foot space on the twenty-sixth floor of a proposed high-rise building bounded by C and B Streets, and Eighth and Ninth Avenues. According to the *Los Angeles*

Times, "Its nearest competition would come from the Symphony Towers project to be built one block north on B Street, where construction barricades have recently been erected."[6]

"The biggest problem with the Financial Gateway issue was the sheer cost of it," said Bixler. According a memorandum from Mathew Spathas at Trammell Crow, the total cost would equal $2,319,175 and did not include any allocation required for parking or further building design changes.

"We would have been required to sign a long-term agreement and pay a minimum of $2 million," said Bixler. "Those who fought against the move to Symphony Towers wanted to stay put or create a new member-owned Club. I had a hard time reconciling either of these alternatives simply on a financial basis."

The dissonance with the "Card Room Gang" reached the point that the Board had to make a substantial peace offering. "We asked them to submit four names of their choosing and two would be included on the new University Club Board of Directors," said Bixler. "Quinn Hornaday and Chuck Cheney were selected."

Bixler recalls the meeting in vivid detail, "The discussion did not go smoothly. I sat directly across from Hornaday, who was the most vicious and least informed. They questioned my authority and responsibilities toward the membership. As the immediate past President, I told them that my primary responsibilities were to ensure the Club's existence now and in the future; to first make sure that the legal debts were paid; and to have a profitable Club; after that we could do what the members wanted. In Hornaday's mind, the correct order was

---

THE CARD ROOM GANG

The Card Room Gang, as they were known, was a group of influential old-timers who spent many a day playing poker in the University Club Card Room. There were two card tables that sat six apiece and a wall buzzer to summon a waiter at a moments' notice. They would bring their own lunches but afterwards head to the bar. The official roster of the Card Room Gang included: John Butler, Thomas Cosgrove, Roy Erwin, Ferdinand Fletcher, Albert Harutunian Jr., Quinn Hornaday, Edgar Luce, Keith Lister, Paul Nielson, Peter Peckham, J. Harold "Bud" Peterson, Klaus Radelow, George Sterling, Dr. Chester Tancredi, and William Wallace.

to satisfy the member's desires first, beyond all else. He wasn't considering the cost of doing business and after two terms as President, having managed to accomplish two consecutive profitable years (the previous fifteen years the Club had operated in the red), I had to give them the financial truth. In the end, it was Cheney who understood it. He said, 'Well, that's plain, we have to move'. It was a turning point as I knew Cheney would go back to the Card Room Gang and get others on board."

"It was about six months or so before the idea was floated to the membership," said Gildred. "We had a luncheon with the membership." The membership was split into two camps—those who saw the future of the Club and those who thought the deal would harm the Club.

"I'll never forget that meeting—it was mid-August and a hotter-than-hell ninety-five degrees when we hosted the Club get-to-know the developer with a Q&A," adds Wilson.

"There were passionate appeals on both sides but in the end the biggest dissenting voice still belonged to Quinn Hornaday," said Gildred. "Some of those who I am close to didn't support the project."

"From my viewpoint," added Gildred, "we were lucky enough to sell the Seventh Avenue building for the amount of money that we did. It was not in good shape and needed asbestos abatement." After residing in the same location since 1916, the second University Clubhouse on Seventh and A Street was sold to San Diego Bar Association in 1989 for slightly more than $836,000.

"My philosophy was that we were full steam ahead for the Symphony Towers Club run by ClubCorp," said Gildred. "We discussed the possibility of continuing the member-owned Club, but Doug said no, so that was that." In the end it was reported that more than three hundred members moved to become members of the new Club bringing the membership to eight hundred by the June 23, 1989 opening gala. Gildred was made Chairman of the new Board of Governors.

According to Tom Blair's column in the *San Diego Union*, "Six weeks after its opening, the stunning new University Club Atop Symphony Towers is just 26 shy of its goal of 850 charter members. That's about double the membership of the old University Club. Initiation fees of $1,000 go to $1,200 next month.[7]

The Financial Gateway project had also been tossed aside; Newman resigned his presidency in protest. That cleared the way for the proposal that included all University Club members to transfer over to the Symphony Towers Club without any initiation fee.

Key players in the University Club Atop Symphony Towers at the opening event. Left to right: William Adair, Phil Gildred, Paul Richey, Doug Wilson, and guest.

"This project was very big and complicated with many ups and downs, but at the end of the day, it is still perceived as the highest quality mixed-use project in the city," said Douglas Wilson, Chairman and CEO of Douglas Wilson Companies.

"The venerable University Club is getting a new home, high above downtown San Diego atop Symphony Towers, and with it a new future. From left are club officers Robert G. Scott, President; Jack E. Deal, Manager of the new operation; and Phillip L. Gildred Jr., a past President of the Club who is Chairman of the new Club's Board of Governors." (*San Diego Evening Tribune*, page C1, May 29, 1989) *Photo by Dana Fisher. Photo courtesy of U-T San Diego*

Grand Opening Party, Sefton Library Ribbon Cutting, 1989. Left to right: Paul Richey, Thomas W. Sefton, and Douglas Wilson. *Courtesy of ClubCorp*

Marilyn Quayle, Helen Copley, and Vice President Dan Quayle.

Lynn Gildred, Thomas Sefton, and Phil Gildred Jr. at the Grand Opening Party. *Courtesy of ClubCorp*

Gordon Luce, Marilyn Quayle, Karon Luce, and Vice President Dan Quayle in 1989.

Kathleen and Douglas Wilson in October 1999.

Charles "Kim" Fletcher and Marilyn Fletcher (right) talk with guests in October 1999.

Leah Swearingen, Phyllis Kraus, and Reba Brophy in October 1999.

Postcard of new University Club entrance and sitting room, 1989.

Main Dining Room, 1989.

New dining room at the Symphony Towers Club as featured in the *San Diego Union*, August 27, 1989. *Photo by Jerry McClard. Photo courtesy of U-T San Diego*

LEFT: Photo of the new Sefton Library, 1989.

AN ICONIC STRUCTURE

One of San Diego's iconic structures, the mixed-use development has a 60,000-square-foot Sky Lobby that spans the entire city block and connects the office tower with the hotel lobby flanking the theater.

According to Wilson, "We donated the entire theater to the San Diego Symphony and then designed 1.1 million square feet around and over Symphony Hall." The building took two years construction time. The team hired the world-class architectural firm Skidmore, Owings & Merrill (SOM).

The thirty-four-story, 625,000-square-foot granite and glass office tower would fronts B Street, while on A Street would is a twenty-seven-story hotel space with 264 guest rooms, meeting and conference facilities, and hotel health club. Five parking levels above the theater accommodates 667 cars connected the two towers. Four parking elevators and thirteen office elevators serve each facet of the building, including the private club on the top floor.

"Unheard of in San Diego, but true, we had the 1.1 million-square-foot, mixed-use building 50-percent leased before we broke ground," said Wilson. The office building held a ribbon cutting in May 1989. From inception to lease up it took five years. I am proud that I survived it." Top companies such as AT&T, KPMG Peat Marwick, Price Waterhouse, Gibson Dunn & Crutcher, and the Fourth Appellate Court of Appeal were among the first to move into the building.

Wilson was recently asked why he did not build a concrete wall surrounding the helipad located on

The lobby of Symphony Towers has an eighty-foot-long, thirteen-foot-high mural called *Symphonic Nuance*. It took Denver artist James Jackson six months to complete this work. *Used with permission of The Irvine Company.*

the roof of Symphony Towers like so many other downtown buildings. "When the FAA advised us that our height restriction for the building was 499 feet, that's where we started our design and worked downward from there," said Wilson. He had not seen the helipad in twenty-five years. "Nothing like taking a walk down memory lane. This building is actually twenty-five years old this year," he adds. "And that's hard to believe."

Symphony Towers was named the 1994 International Office Building of the Year in its class by Building Owners and Managers Association (BOMA) International.

Today, the Symphony Towers office tower is managed by Irvine Company Office Properties.

ABOVE: Club advertisement featuring Dr. Mark Irwin Jacobs. *Courtesy of ClubCorp*

LEFT: Club advertisement featuring John Moores. *Courtesy of ClubCorp*

ENDNOTES

1. Lucinda Eddy, "Visions of Paradise, the Selling of San Diego." Horton Plaza Redevelopment Project," *The Journal of San Diego History*, San Diego Historical Society Quarterly, Summer 1995, Volume 41, Number 3.

2. Greg Joseph, "University Club, Up from Limbo to the top of Symphony Towers," *San Diego Evening Tribune*, May 29, 1989, pp. C1–3.

3. Bullard Thornton, Sally. "An Atmosphere of Friendliness, The Cuyamaca Club." *The Journal of San Diego History*, San Diego Historical Society Quarterly, Fall 1983, Volume 29, Number 4.

4. Greg Joseph, "University Club, Up from Limbo to the top of Symphony Towers," *San Diego Evening Tribune*, May 29, 1989, pp. C1–3.

5. "Step Back/University Club," *San Diego Union-Tribune*, August 27, 1989, p. F-38.

6. "San Diego County Digest," *Los Angeles Times*, November 22, 1986.

7. Tom Blair column, *San Diego Union*, August 23, 1989, p. B-1.

A HOME FOR THE SAN DIEGO SYMPHONY

"IT WAS IN THE MID-1980S WHEN BOTH the San Diego Symphony and the San Diego Opera performed at the Civic Center," according to Linc Ward, former member of the San Diego Symphony Board. The San Diego Symphony was floundering and close to bankruptcy. While across town the San Diego Opera was flourishing. "I recall that the Tito Cocobiana, managing head of the Opera, started booking performances three years in advance which prevented the Symphony from playing a full 'season'," said Ward. "We had to find a new venue but we didn't have any money." Ward, along with Michael "Det" Merryman, President of the San Diego Symphony (1984–86) and Rancho Santa Fe entrepreneur Blain Quick worked quickly when they saw that there was an option to buy an entire city block including the Fox Theater, but the group needed pledges to buy the option. Ward, who was head of Pacific Bell, along with Hal Sadler, President of Mission Federal, pledged $50,000 apiece. Blaine acquired the option and met with Douglas Wilson with provisions that the Fox Theater would be kept, and that the office building and hotel would be built around the theater, and that the Symphony's new home would be called Symphony Hall and that the Symphony would receive a small override of the building's rental income. "This move saved the San Diego Symphony," said Ward. "We ended up with a new performance space, parking, and minor income from Symphony Towers tenants."

LEFT: Copley Symphony Hall in 2013. *Photo: ZackBenson.com*

TOP RIGHT: Copley Symphony Hall Lobby. *Used with permission of The Irvine Company. © The Irvine Company LLC 2014. All rights reserved*

BOTTOM RIGHT: Doreen Whiney and Mstislav Rostropovich at the Symphony Opening Dinner Gala at the University Club Atop Symphony Towers in 1990s.

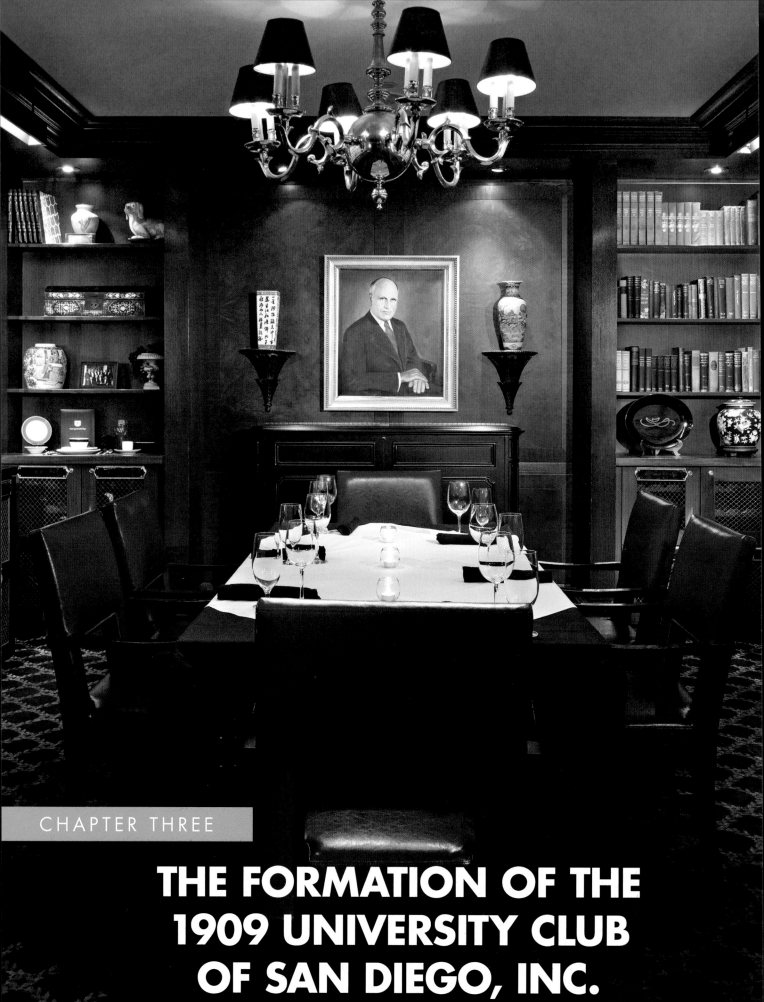

CHAPTER THREE

THE FORMATION OF THE 1909 UNIVERSITY CLUB OF SAN DIEGO, INC.

THE UNIVERSITY CLUB ON SEVENTH AVENUE, CIRCA 1984

It is human nature to seek out social opportunities and a place where there is a sense of belonging. This is especially true in an urban setting with a higher density of professional workers. In the 1970s there were three private city clubs in San Diego whose membership had been started by the families whose ancestors had settled in San Diego in the late 1800s and early 1900s. By the 1980s the University Club was the only remaining one.

Although the University Club Clubhouse on Seventh Avenue and Ash Street was not nearly as attractive as Symphony Towers, those who belonged in the 1970s and 1980s, just as they do in today's Club, enjoyed the full-service facilities, and the opportunity to conduct business, to socialize, and to attend meetings and educational seminars featuring prominent leaders in government and business. The athletic facilities were also a draw for many—and all with ample, free parking available.

One of the most appreciated member benefits was being a part of a worldwide Club network.

The University Club maintained reciprocity with ninety-seven clubs in metropolitan markets such as New York University Club, The Press Club of San Francisco, the Cosmos Club of Washington, D.C., and the University Club of Chicago. International club reciprocity included a network of twenty clubs in twelve countries including Mexico, Canada, Argentina, England, Scotland, Australia, New Zealand, Hong Kong, Japan, South Africa, Sri Lanka, and Sweden. Wherever members traveled, they could stay in comfortable home-away-from-home surroundings.

There were also a plethora of interesting events held at the Club including diplomatic dinners, mayoral receptions, award ceremonies, and speaker's seminars. Members hosted murder mystery dinners

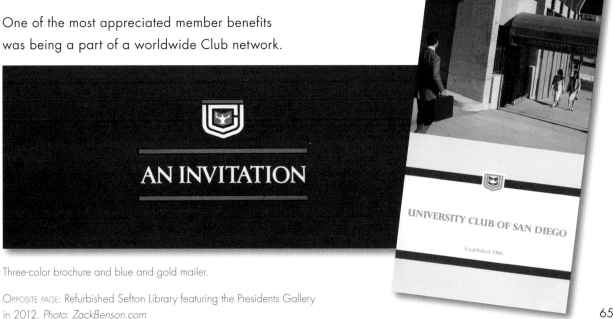

AN INVITATION

UNIVERSITY CLUB OF SAN DIEGO

Established 1906

Three-color brochure and blue and gold mailer.

OPPOSITE PAGE: Refurbished Sefton Library featuring the Presidents Gallery in 2012. *Photo: ZackBenson.com*

which used multiple rooms, and an antique car show, hosted by member Bill Evans who loaned several cars from his private collection. Members also took trips such as watching the America's Cup races, a bus trip to Laguna, and a fourteen-day European tour.

"I recall two especially memorable events," said Ann Beard, University Club President 1996–1998 and the Club's Social Director in 1985. "One when historian Ken Kramer emceed a lavish Monte Carlo night to benefit the San Diego Master Chorale, and the second when we honored the then-new Mayor, Susan Golding. This was personally meaningful as I had just been appointed the Chief of Protocol for the City of San Diego."

Club membership included more than one hundred people who were part of employer or company memberships. The largest employer groups belonged to San Diego Trust & Savings Bank with twenty-six, San Diego Gas & Electric Company with twenty, and Great American First Savings & Loan with sixteen members.

Many respected organizations such as the World Trade Center, UCSD Connect, LEAD San Diego, CONVIS, and the International Sister City organization held regular events at the Club. In addition members celebrated holidays, birthdays, and family milestones. Annual traditions were formed such as the Annual Egg Nog party and President's Dinner traditions.

In honor of the Club's Seventy-fifth Anniversary, members and their guests arrived in vintage automobiles and dressed as if they had just stepped out of a 1909 issue of *Harper's Bazaar* with top hats on the gents and long gowns for the ladies. Also that night, the San Diego Padres were playing the Detroit Tigers in the World Series, so even though everyone was dressed as if it were 1909, they watched the baseball game on the wide-screen television.[1]

The most prestigious event each year was the Annual President's Ball. Guests arrived in black tie for a Monte Carlo, Casino Royale, or a Valentine-themed evening. In 1984 Mike Bixler expanded the Presidents' events to include a President's Luncheon. "For the first lunch we honored the oldest living President, 1937 University Club President Dr. Chester Tanner. Lou Garday, University Club President 1981, emceed the event and after a full introduction said, 'I present to you Dr. Chester Tanner'—the room was in total silence as the ninety-year-old Tanner had fallen asleep (at least that is what we all hoped), so Garday raised his voice and repeated, 'I present to you Dr. Chester Tanner, to which, Tanner awoke instantly, gave a thumbs up sign and said 'right on'—the room erupted in laughter, and I dare say, I bit of relief," recounts Bixler.

A popular annual family event included the Laurel and Hardy Movie Night. San Diego Trust & Savings Bank CEO Thomas Sefton co-hosted the event along with popcorn king Orville Redenbacher. As one of the country's foremost collector of Laurel and Hardy films, Sefton supplied the movies. The night usually started with hotdogs and hamburgers and entertainment from Club member George Harris and his renowned Yankee Air Pirates Dixieland Band. And, the University Club's Men's Glee first performed at the original "Movie Night" organized by then President, Bill Hiscock.

"It was on one of those stormy Movie Nights that Sefton offered to have his chauffeur pick up my son from home so that he could enjoy Laurel and Hardy comedies as well," said Beard. "You only find that kind of thoughtfulness and camaraderie in a private club."

From left to right: Chuck Cheney, Rob Scott, and Dr. Michael Clarke.

Members seated left to right: Dr. Michael Clarke, Mike Bixler, Stan Keniston, and Sally Bixler.

Jim Haugh and Bill Hiscock.

Holiday Issue

University Club of San Diego

1333 Seventh Avenue   **Vol. XV, No. 9**   **Telephone 233-6606**

Newsletter

Club members celebrate the 75th Anniversary in full regalia as Stan Keniston, Rob Scott, Bill and Nikki Hiscock, Mike Bixler and guests get the party "rolling" with their vintage automobile, a 1914 Overland.

University Club's 75th Anniversary Celebration

Seventy-five years and still going strong! The University Club of San Diego honored itself with a birthday party, Friday, October 12, attended by a good mixture of Club members. To accentuate this historical event, Club President **William Hiscock** and his wife **Nikki**, as well as **Mike Bixler** (Vice President), new members **Stan Keniston** and **Rob Scott** and their guests, arrived in vintage automobiles. All dressed as if they had just stepped out of a 1909 issue of "Harper's Bazaar," with top hats for the gents and long gowns for the ladies. Many Club photos and memorabilia were displayed for the event, encouraging all to walk down "Memory Lane."

Concurrently, history was being made as our San Diego Padres played the Detroit Tigers in a World Series game. **Rick Golding** (Club Manager) arranged for us to follow the game by way of the Club's wide-screen television, so no action was lost!

Among members present were **Dr.** and **Mrs. Walter Porter, George** and **Joanne Harris, Bill** and **Mildred Walsh** (who stopped by for dinner and a glimpse of the game on their way to the Opera). **Eunis Christensen, Edward Whitney, Joy Poncie, Bill** and **Christine Neitfeld** and new members **Dr. & Mrs. Robert Desmond; Suzanne Swift, Bill** and **Eileen Holliday, Leonard Dodson, Gene MacFarland, Gary** and **Pat Sullivan** with their children **Charlotte** and **David; Mark Roberts, Jane Ellen Davis, Dr. George Ellis, Ruth Krinjeck, Willard Hage, Jack** and **Barbara Pontius, Mario Palomino, Dr.** and **Mrs. Bernard Novis** and **Lee Otsubo.**

Former Club presidents in attendance were **Jere** and **Mary Lien** and **Philip** and **Lyn Gildred.**

Warm Up For The Holidays at the Club

Dinner Is Served Thursday and Friday Evenings ...

We have a fresh new dinner menu each Thursday and Friday night, featuring the Chef's special.

As the Holidays approach, use the Club as your starting point for an evening out or as an opportunity to meet other Club members.

Reserve Early For This Season's Party Planning ...

Plan your social events at the Club this holiday season. Our catering staff is ready to create a gourmet meal with all the trimmings, made especially for your private event. Or choose from a variety of delicious offerings on the Club's menu. Invite guests to join you at a Club lunch or dinner, featuring holiday favorites guaranteed to put everyone in seasonal cheer.

We hope you will schedule office parties, cocktail get-togethers and other functions at the Club. Our extended schedule will allow you to accommodate these celebrations particularly during Christmas week. Private meeting rooms are available for groups. Call Laurie or Lynette at 233-6606 for reservations and assistance.

Friday Buffets

If you haven't already joined us for our Friday Buffet, be sure to join us for an assortment of delicious entrees, salads and desserts. The Club's Chef prepares this magnificent buffet every Friday through the end of the year from 11:30 a.m. to 2 p.m. Reservations are suggested as the buffet is always popular.

(continued on page 7)

Cover for 75th Anniversary in 1985.

CLUB PHOTOS

Sharing stories of the past and plans for the future, Dr. Robert Desmond, Tom Sefton and Bill Nietfeld joined in the evening's celebration.

Dressed the part, in vintage 1920's "gladrags," Bill and Nikki Hiscock teamed up to blow out the Club's 75th birthday cake.

Christine Nietfeld and Emily Desmond enjoyed a special Anniversary dinner in the main dining room.

Club members Phil Gildred and Tom Sefton came to share the festivities with fellow members and catch the Padres action on wide-screen tv.

UNIVERSITY CLUB

Page 5 photos for 75th Anniversary.

THE MEN'S GLEE— A MUSICAL TRADITION

"Most commonly called 'The Glee' we wore blue blazers with the Club 'Lamp of Learning' logo on the breast pocket and straw bowler hats," said Rob Scott, University Club President in 1989–1990 and 2006–2007 and Glee Club founder. "We performed at the Club and around town, mostly Barbershop songs, College Glee, but also traditional and classical numbers."

The Men's Glee Club was formed in 1984 with "charter members" Mike Bixler, Bill Hiscock, and Rob Scott. Jim Alcorn, Don Swall, Larry Wade, Stan Keniston, Lee Plat, Bill Templeton, Michael Clark, and Aubry Thompson soon joined them. They sang one night a week in the card room, which was intentionally situated close to the Club's bar. During the Holidays, they honed their singing chops on Christmas Carols. The wives of the Glee members formed their own tradition at the Club with an annual Christmas Lunch. That Holiday Lunch tradition continues still today by the women of the 1909 Board of Directors: Barbara Alcorn, Ann Beard, Sally Bixler, Suzanne Swift, and Julie Walke.

"The first time we sang most of the songs with hat in hand for theatrical effect," said Scott. "It should be noted that the then-to-be-memorized music was hidden inside the crown of the hat which gave additional purpose to the bare-headed singing."

Some of the Glee's favorite songs were: *Aura Lee, Gaudeamus Igitur, Men of Harlech, Once in Our Lives Let Us Drink to Our Wives, The Pope—He Leads A Jolly Life, Death is a Long, Long Sleep*, and *Good King Wenceslas* just to name a few.

Men's Glee—The Early Days: Aubry Thompson, Stan Keniston, Rob Scott, Mike Bixler, Don Swall, and Bill Hiscock relaxing before a performance in Coronado.

Men's Glee Performance at the Monte Carlo Event at the Symphony Towers Club, April 9, 1999.

Remaining members of the Men's Glee at the 2012 Sefton Library Reopening. Left to right: Rob Scott, Mike Bixler, Stan Keniston, Jim Alcorn, and Bill Hiscock.

At the end of the rehearsal, by virtue of the proximity to the bar, the Glee's rehearsals appeared more like a "Stag Night." In fact, the Glee hosted an official "Stag Night" for Mike Bixler before he wed Sally Allen. "We had dinner at the Hob Nob Hill restaurant in Banker's Hill and headed downtown to close a bar or two with our singing," recalls Scott. "We all piled into the 'Glee-mobile', which in reality was Bixler's 1962 Lincoln convertible with the top down. It was a hoot!"

The Glee went on to perform at the Elks Club, Hotel del Coronado, a Coronado retirement home, and more than once in the Coronado Fourth of July parade. "Parades were easy," said Scott. "We could sing the same song over as our audience kept changing down the road." Scott recalls a lesson well learned, "At a retirement home I learned that you don't perform what you have not rehearsed. Once we asked a new piano player to accompany us and at one point, he was so far ahead of our singing that I had to march over to him as if it were choreography, put my hands on top of his hands, until the singers caught up. Fortunately the audience was forgiving."

The Glee also performed at the Symphony Towers Club. "We held command performances at the Presidents' Galas and at the Egg Nog Party. We also sang at the funerals of member Lee Platt and Larry Wade's father," added Scott.

The members of the Men's Glee forged friendships and celebrated personal milestone. "One particularly memorable birthday party was for Bixler's fiftieth where Aubry Thompson donned a judge's wig and held an impromptu trial over trumped-up charges of conduct unbecoming a Mayor (Bixler was Mayor of the City of Imperial Beach). Attorney Hiscock unsuccessfully defended Bixler against an onslaught of witnesses and tainted evidence," said Scott. "In revenge, Bixler helped orchestrate the celebration of Thompson's eightieth. At that event where we all appeared dressed as angels to inform Thompson that he had to atone for much sinning with little time left in which accomplish it."

"As with all great singers such as Luciano Pavarotti, age leads to retirement and the Glee Club and its activities are a fond memory," sighs Scott.

STORM CLOUDS GATHERING

"It was important to us all to have a quality City Club like other big cities," said Mike Bixler, who was President in 1985 and 1986. A prominent, vibrant, and prestigious city club is a hallmark of a World Class City. But as mentioned earlier, private clubs were not thriving as one would hope and the University Club, despite its long history and highly attended events, was also experiencing sustainability problems.

"I will never forget the day when I discovered a list of vendors who hadn't been paid for a couple of years," said Bixler. "I was horrified. I asked the accounts payable person to send a note of apology and start making small, monthly, good faith payments to vendors. In this way, they would know that we were intent on living up to our obligations."

Bixler was known about the Club as a hands-on President, "Every day, I walked over for lunch and invited the General Manager to sit down and discuss day-to-day issues. "The finances were dismal and much of the employee relations issues could be attributed to workers staying there too long when

71

A Monthly Newsletter for Members

MAY 1989

University Club of San Diego

Present Clubhouse Building To Close June 30th, 1989

Club address since 1916

For 73 years the University Club of San Diego has remained at the 7th & A Street location. It was moved to the present address in 1916, seven years after its birth.

The current clubhouse building was constructed in 1970; a few months shy of 20 years ago.

The new Club facilities on the 34th floor atop Symphony Towers is scheduled to open mid-June.

The existing clubhouse has not been sold (as of this writing). All Club operations will cease June 30th, 1989 and the present club building will be closed.

Club members who have lockers in the spa are requested to remove all of their personal belongings by Friday, June 30th.

The dining room (located in the lounge), card room, library, bar and meeting rooms will be available for any and all fuctions.

An auction and farewell party will be held May 5th. Under separate cover you have been sent an invitation. We are planning a most enjoyable evening. One you won't want to miss. Your 1909 costume may be a prize winner!

The books in the library and the many interesting items in the rummage room will be on sale starting Monday, April 24th. First come, first gets best choice.

The latest information we have from those working on the new Club

facilities is that the new quarters will be opening the middle of June.

As the affairs of the Club are being put in order, it is imperative that your account be paid in full. Please send us your check now so that we may close the Club books in a timely manner.

Jack Deal Appointed New Club Manager

Mr. Jack Deal has been appointed Club manager of the University Club. He will be the manager in the new quarters scheduled to open in the middle of June.

Prior to joining the University Club, Mr. Deal was with Fess Parker's Red Lion Resort in Santa Barbara. He was the Director of Food and Beverage service.

He has been receiving special management orientation from Club Corporation of America at the Centre Club in Costa Mesa prior to his coming to San Diego.

Until the new Club quarters open, Mr. Deal's temporary office is in the current Clubhouse with the current membership office.

Mr. Deal, 40 and single, is familiar with elegant service and is looking forward to serving the members and guests of the 80-year-old University Club of San Diego.

they should have moved on to other jobs," said Bixler. "There was an underlying pressure to come up with a solution because we were fast becoming the place where the 'elite meet but not to eat'."

Measures had to be taken toward Club solvency, which meant the loss of a well-liked General Manager who wouldn't conform to charging room rates and hospitality fees for longtime member associations. "You simply cannot run a business by giving away the things that would have provided a profit, and in the end, I was accountable to the membership," said Bixler.

After fifteen continuous years of losing money, Bixler points to a proud accomplishment, "During my tenure

as president the Club made a profit and it helped prolong the life of the club. But we quickly realized that it would be difficult to attract new membership based on competition from restaurants that had views. We had reached the point where the dining room, which was twelve feet above the sidewalk, was not a draw."

"If the truth be told, the nexus of us looking skyward for a dining experience, started on the evening that we hosted a Board of Directors dinner on our roof," said Bixler. "The table was set for twelve and as we watched, twilight turned into evening and the city lights came up around us. That visual impact was the turning point in which the Board of Directors started thinking about the Club in a new, more grandiose, way."

Newsletter June 1989—May 5 auction.

OPPORTUNITY OF A LIFETIME

"So when the opportunity arose for us to move to the top of Symphony Towers, I was delighted that we could ensure the survival of the University Club in a prestigious and dignified way—to have a fine City Club again," said Bixler.

"I wasn't opposed to the move," said Scott whose presidency followed the abrupt departure of Attorney Barry Newman whose alternative Clubhouse proposal was rejected by the membership (see Chapter Two). After Newman's successor William Conrad fulfilled the remainder of Newman's term, the only contested election for President in the Club's history was held in 1989 in which Bob Rideout ran for the loyal opposition against the then-Board Vice President Scott. Fortunately, the dissenters did not prevail, and the newly elected Scott concluded the meeting in an

The University Club of San Diego sells building to the State Bar Association. Rob Scott (left) and Mike Bixler accept a very large check.

atmosphere of respect and courtesy. In the end, Scott's detractors subsequently joined the rest of the membership at the Symphony Towers Club.

"I felt that I should remain neutral," adds Scott. "Whenever challenged by a member, who didn't want to make the move, I would say, 'Go into the dining room and take a look at the curtains; they are in terrible shape'."

On May 5, 1989, Club members held a final auction party to divest themselves from the furniture and fixtures. While committee members dressed in period clothing, auctioneer Bob Arnyhm handled the final sales. The official day of closing on June 30, 1989, was marked by a final toast celebrated by 140 members who honored the Eightieth Anniversary with eighty-cent drinks.[2]

SELLING THE OLD BUILDING

Club Manager Bob Crouch was known for having a great sense of humor and a flair for the dramatic. The day that escrow closed, Crouch arranged for a Board meeting to be held at the title company. A faux check was presented to Board members, however the check was immediately stolen by a mysterious "cleaning lady" who just so happened to be dusting the room during the check presentation. A chase ensued, with Board members following the rather large, rather hairy cleaner. Both parties ended up at Sea World where the check coincidentally crossed the stage in the hands of a show performer with a University Club Board member in hot pursuit. All was resolved at a dinner, but the point had been made that this was a memorable occasion. Not simply over the antics, but because it signified for the first time since 1916 that the University Club of San Diego no longer owned a Clubhouse.

SYMPHONY TOWERS RISES

"None of us will forget the bone-jarring pounding that shook our building and jolted the water glasses in the dining room while Symphony Towers was being built," said Beard.

"The noise was well worth it, because the Board of Directors had the rare opportunity to take a construction tour to the top of the construction," said Scott. "It was very memorable."

"I will never forget wearing a hardhat and hanging on for dear life aboard the rickety construction elevator as it climbed the outside of the building up to the thirty-fourth floor," adds Beard. "The view was positively breathtaking looking past the concrete and steel girders at the sailboats and city lights while the wind whipped our faces. We were standing in the triangular overhang now known as the 'Apollo Room' *without windows.* Now, that is what I call an open bar!"

Egg Nog Party 1997. Left to right: Don Swall, Sally Bixler, Ann Beard, Suzanne Swift, Rob Scott, and Julie Walke.

THE 1909 LEGACY BOARD IS ESTABLISHED

After the move, some of the members of the transition committee became the new Board of Directors of the newly named 1909 University Club of San Diego, Inc., whose aim was to maintain some of the old Club traditions such as the Egg Nog Party and the annual President's Dinner at the Symphony Towers location.

1997 Egg Nog Party. Left to right: Barbara and James Alcorn, Olga McCord, Bill Hiscock, Mike Bixler, and Phil Gildred.

THE ANNUAL EGG NOG PARTY TOAST

Written by Club Historian Charles "Charley" Pinco, 1879–1975

- ⚜ Again we meet for revel and laughter— for Christmas cheer and what comes after—but for the present, its Egg Nog and Holly, forgetting about other concerns and our folly.

- ⚜ So let the Wassail cup be drained—a health to our friends unrestrained.

- ⚜ Let our wishes be like burning embers, A Happy New Year to our Fellow Members!

1909 Board of Directors at the 2012 Egg Nog Party. Left to right: Rob Scott, Suzanne Swift, Don Fine, Julie Walke, Jim Alcorn, and Ann Beard.

HONORING EDUCATORS

In the 1990s, the 1909 Board continued to conduct business at the subsequent Symphony Towers Club. Stanley F. Keniston was elected in 1992 and served two one-year terms. He was followed as President by Michael Clark in 1994 also for two one-year terms. Both Keniston and Clark were the driving force behind the Honors Program.

The Honors Program was designed to recognize less-known leaders in education, art, or business, who contributed to making a difference in the lives of those less fortunate. At the first program in 1994 the Club recognized Celia Ballesteros, Esq., Board member, Centro Cultural de la Raza; Marti Lipovsky, President, San Diego City College Foundation; Margaret Iwanaga Penrose, Union of Pan Asian Communities; Harry C. Weinberg, Ed.D., CSU San Marcos; and Shirley Williams, Executive Director, African American Museum of Fine Arts. Honorees were presented with $1,000 honorarium.

In the 1995 Honors Program, Ernst Clark Griffin, Ph.D., San Diego State, Department of Geography; Candice Lopez, San Diego City College, Graphic Arts Department; and Holly Eissler Given, Ph.D., UCSD Scripps Institution of Oceanography, were honored for their contributions to education and to the community-at-large.

University Club History Hall.

THE FIRST FEMALE PRESIDENT

"University education was paramount in my family," said Beard, the first female President. "For generations my family in Colorado has supported higher education and the arts. My dad, a world traveler, graduated from Harvard Law School, my granddad from Columbia University Law, and my grandmother from Wellesley College."
—Ann Beard

In 1996, Ann Southard Beard was elected the first woman President since the 1909 incorporation of the University Club of San Diego, Inc.

"President Mike Bixler and Rob Scott hired me as Social Director in 1986 to replace the retiring Mary McMillen," said Beard. "With a background in business marketing, I was a natural fit to promote the Club's distinguished heritage of traditions and amenities. Ten years later, in 1996, the Board honored me by electing me its first woman President."

Beard focused her efforts to build a speaker's bureau and to build a scholarship program to

Dedication of the 1909 University Club Room at San Diego State University. Front row, left to right: Julie Walke, Denice Bay, and Suzanne Swift. Middle row, left to right: Rob Scott, SDSU President Stephen Weber, University Club President Ann Beard, SDSU Athletic Director Rick Bay, and Mike Bixler. Back row, left to right: Earl Ligon, Bill Adair, unidentified, Don Fine, Jim Alcorn, and Bill Hiscock.

This room is named in honor of

The 1909 University Club of San Diego

in recognition of their generous support for the SDSU library

The following individuals have also donated additional gifts to this project

Rick & Denice Bay
Dallas Clark
Keith & Myrna Hall
J.W. Sefton Foundation

William H. Adair
Ann S. Beard
Gretchen Kier Bennett
Mayor & Mrs. Michael B. Bixler
Georgia C. Borthwick
Gail A. Burnett
Michael J. Clark
J. Frederick Conrad
Donald E. Fine

George Lewis Gildred
Philip L. Gildred, Jr.
Carlos David Malamud
Frieda H. Morgenstern
Robert G. Scott
Donald T. Swall
Suzanne L. Swift
William E. Temple
Aubrey F. Thompson
Julie M. Walke

award academic excellence. The 1909 Board invested in the development of a conference room, named after the 1909 University Club of San Diego, in the Love Library complex at San Diego State University. The conference room houses a

> **DID YOU KNOW...**
>
> The first one-hundredth-anniversary celebration took place on October 12, 1996, to commemorate the start of the College Graduate Club in 1896. The new Symphony Towers Club had reached a total of 1,123 members.

portion of the art and artifacts collection. In addition to the Board's donation, there were several individuals who contributed to the project. They included Rick and Denice Bay, Dallas Clark, Keith and Myrna Hall, and the J. W. Sefton Foundation.

In April 1999, Ann Beard was recognized for her outstanding leadership and dedication to the University Club, for hosting the first One Hundredth

Anniversary Celebration in 1996, and for her two-year Presidency of the 1909 Board of Directors.

The vision of the 1909 University Club Board continued to draw on the resources and heritage of the old University Club with its mission to direct activities toward protecting and enhancing the legacy, traditions, and assets while working in cooperation with the University Club Atop Symphony Towers and finally, to provide a club and organization worthy of our membership.[3]

ESTABLISHING A PLACE IN HISTORY

In 2008, Julie M. Walke was elected the second woman President. Walke, with her penchant for details, reviewed the fundamentals of the finances, investments, bylaws, and assets. As a result several paintings belonging to the art collection were restored and reframed in advance of the works hanging in the new gallery as a part of the Club's reinvention.

Only two women have been University Club President: Ann Beard (right) served from 1996 to 1998 and ten years later Julie Walke was elected in 2008 and is still serving in that capacity. *Photo by Melissa Jacobs*

One-hundredth Anniversary Black Tie and Blue Jeans event to benefit the Lamp of Learning Scholarship Fund. Left to right: Rob Scott, Mike Bixler, Suzanne Swift, Don Fine, Julie Walke, and Tommy Trause.

CURRENTS&ARTS

SECTION **E**

Ann, Abby 2
Don Freeman 2
InStyle 3
Television 6
Comics 7-8

THE SAN DIEGO UNION-TRIBUNE • MONDAY, OCTOBER 14, 1996

SAN DIEGO HISTORICAL SOCIETY / Photos

Lounge lizards: *Starting in 1916, University Club members repaired to the lounge at their clubhouse, where the men-only group ate 35-cent steak dinners and rented apartments for $1.50 per day.*

Century *of* Tradition

University Club has evolved with city itself

By Roger M. Showley
STAFF WRITER

Eight men and 13 women met for the first time 100 years ago this month in San Diego to speak of many things.

Of English coinage and evolution, of race relations and "certain recognized mental differences" between men and women.

Members of the College Graduate Club rotated the role of "essayist" every other Thursday evening. Following a 20-minute presentation, each member had five minutes to respond to the topic; spouses could participate in the discussions but could not vote on club business.

A college degree from one of 35 recognized institutions was required. (The University of California's only campus, in Berkeley, and Stanford University were the only eligible

California colleges. San Diego had no liberal arts colleges.)

Dues were just 50 cents per year. But if you missed two consecutive meetings, you were out.

Today, the conversation and setting are quite different at the University Club Atop Symphony Towers downtown.

While taking in the breathtaking views of San Diego Bay from the 34th floor, the 1,150 members of the University Club consult the extensive wine list, sample the tasty dessert tray and take phone calls at their tables.

Initiation is $1,200; monthly dues are $97. You need one club sponsor and two personal references to join, and no one has yet been turned away.

And by the way, don't worry about your al-

See **CLUB** *on Page E-4*

Landmark no more: *Designed by club member William S. Hebbard, the University Club was demolished to make way for a 1970 replacement at Seventh Avenue and A Street. The San Diego County Bar Association now occupies the building.*

THE ART COLLECTION

The 1909 University Club of San Diego has a small, but significant, fine art collection. It includes some of the most interesting Southern California artists of the early twentieth century. The works were donated in the 1920s and 1930s by prominent members. Also included are historical items kept from earlier Clubhouses. Some of the paintings can be seen in historic photos of the Club.

Sunset on El Cajon (El Capitan) by Alfred R. Mitchell (1888–1972).

Laguna Beach by William Alexander Griffith (1866–1940).

Boats of Sottomarina by Edgar Alwin Payne (1882–1947).

Untitled San Diego Landscape, A Mesa and Clouds by Aime Baxter Titus (1883–1941).

Shadow Patterns by Lela J. Titus (1889–1984).

Untitled Yacatan Jungle Scene by Everett Gee Jackson (1900–1995).

Seagulls and Sand Dunes by Walter J. Fenn (1863–circa 1962).

Gallery Hall © Clay Hayner 2011— Courtesy of ClubCorp

"The 1909 Board needed a fresh start and new energy," said Walke. "It was a lot of work but well worth the effort. The Board is more relevant and active." Walke was asked to join the Board of Governors in 2012 and currently serves on the Executive Committee.

"For the past six years our activities have been focused on establishing our place in Club history," said Walke. "We have started to work on Club legacy, through this publication, by participating in the Lamp of Learning Scholarship fund, and by sponsoring the Club Arts Committee at the Symphony Towers Club."

In 2010, after the Club's Reinvention, the 1909 Board took the lead and paid for the newly refurbished Sefton Library and preservation of the Presidents' Gallery. Board Members Bixler and Keniston helped shepherd the process. San Diego historian Rick Crawford was hired to research and write the presidents' biographies. (The biographies are featured in Chapter Four.)

The 1909 University Club Board of Directors is the sponsoring organization for current Club's fine art exhibitions that are installed on a quarterly basis. To date, they have insured the artwork loaned by the La Jolla Athenaeum, Museum of Contemporary Art, Mingei International Museum, San Diego Museum of Art, the Sefton Family Foundation, the Stuart Collection at UCSD, the La Jolla Playhouse, the Oceanside Museum of Art, Ilan Lael Foundation, and the San Diego History Center.

1909 Board of Directors in September 2007. Left to right: Seated are the late Dr. Michael Clark (President 1991 and 2000) and Stan Keniston (President 1992–93) who created the Honors Program. Standing: Mike Bixler, Suzanne Swift, Julie Walke, and President Rob Scott.

THE SEFTON LIBRARY

The Sefton Library was first founded after the University Club was incorporated in 1909. It has stayed as a part of the Clubhouses including the Symphony Towers Club as it was to assure new members of a familiar tie with the past.[1] The room is named after a venerable San Diego banking family who founded San Diego Trust & Savings Bank in 1889. The Seftons are among a handful of city leaders who constructed major buildings in the early 1900s in what has become the Gaslamp Quarter.

Although a Sefton never served as President, the family influence is an important part of our history. The leadership of Joseph W. Sefton Jr., along with the generosity and support of his son, Thomas W. Sefton, helped keep the University Club of San Diego a viable institution during prosperous and lean times. The Sefton Library honors the Sefton family commitment to the University Club and houses a portrait of Joseph W. Sefton Jr. along with the Presidents Collection.

1. Burnett, *The University Club of San Diego—Past and Present*, June 1989, p. 6.

TOP: Past presidents ceremoniously reopen the Sefton Library and the newly installed Presidents Gallery with a ribbon cutting on February 28, 2012. Left to right: Don Fine (2005), Rob Scott (1989–1990, 2006–2007), George Delafield (1976), Julie Walke (2008–2014), Stan Keniston (1992–1993), Ann Beard (1996–1998), Bill Hiscock (1984), Stephen P. Oggel (1980), Mike Bixler (1985–1986), and W. Daniel Larsen (1967) © *Doug Gates Photography*

MIDDLE RIGHT: Left to right: Stephen Oggel and Sally King with Selwyn and George Delafield. © *Doug Gates Photography*

BOTTOM: Mike and Sally Bixler with Scott Hollaender of UBS. © *Doug Gates Photography*

Top: 2013 Annual Meeting. *Photo by Melissa Jacobs*

Left: The women of the 1909 University Club Board of Directors: Vice President Suzanne Swift, President Julie Walke, Recording Secretary Kendall DePascal, and past President Ann Beard. *Photo by Melissa Jacobs*

ENDNOTES

1. University Club Newsletter, Holiday Issue October 1994, Volume 15, Number 9, p. 1.

2. University Club Newsletter, May and June 1989, p. 1.

3. The Vision and Mission Statement of the 1909 University Club of San Diego, Inc., ca. 1995.

CHAPTER FOUR

105 YEARS OF
SAN DIEGO LEADERSHIP

Featuring Presidents' Biographies by San Diego Historian Richard W. Crawford

UNIVERSITY CLUB PRESIDENTS 1909–2014

FOR OVER A CENTURY, THE UNIVERSITY CLUB IN SAN DIEGO HAS BEEN SYNONYMOUS WITH LEADERSHIP AND THOSE THAT HAVE SERVED AS PRESIDENT OF THE CITY'S OLDEST SOCIAL CLUB HAVE SET REMARKABLE STANDARDS OF ACHIEVEMENT IN THEIR CHOSEN PROFESSIONS AND AS COMMUNITY LEADERS. THE RANKS OF UNIVERSITY CLUB PRESIDENTS HAVE ALL BEEN DISTINGUISHED BY THEIR ENERGETIC, PUBLIC-SPIRITED INVOLVEMENT IN THE BETTERMENT OF THE SAN DIEGO COMMUNITY.

—Historian Richard Crawford

RUSSELL C. ALLEN (1909–1910)

Born in 1859 Allen was the son of a Harvard University professor. After graduating from Harvard in 1880, Allen studied law at Columbia but came to California and purchased a ranch in the Sweetwater Valley. Allen's success with raisin growing and olive orchards led to formation of the Sweetwater Fruit Company in 1890. Capital from Boston spurred development and the company specialized in citrus that they shipped throughout the country. Russell Allen was Director of the Buildings and Grounds Committee for the Panama-California Exposition (1915) and was Chairman of the San Diego County Draft Board during World War I. He joined the Cuyamaca Club in 1890 and soon became involved with the College Graduate Club—a precursor to the University Club.

WILLIAM S. HEBBARD (1911)

Noted San Diego architect Hebbard was born in Milford, Michigan, in 1863. Educated in New York, he graduated from the Cornell University School of Architecture in 1887. After a year in Chicago, working for the famed architectural firm of Burnham and Root, Hebbard settled in San Diego in 1890. William Hebbard designed and supervised the construction of many of San Diego's most significant buildings, often with partners. With Carleton M. Winslow, he designed the All Saints Episcopal Church on Sixth and Pennsylvania. With Irving Gill he supervised the construction of San Diego's Carnegie Library building at Eighth and E Streets. Hebbard and Gill would also design and build the State Normal School (San Diego State)

RUSSELL C. ALLEN (1908–1910). *Courtesy Harvard University Archives, HUP Allen, R.C. (1a)*

WILLIAM S. HEBBARD (1911). *© San Diego History Center*

OPPOSITE PAGE: Aerial of Seventh Avenue looking north toward Cortez Hill: The Fox Theater is the prominent building on B Street. Directly to the north just beyond A Street, you can see the white, four-story University Club headquarters designed in 1916 by noted architect William S. Hebbard. *© San Diego History Center*

in University Heights and the George W. Marston House near Balboa Park. He designed the Club's first permanent building: a Spanish Renaissance Clubhouse built in 1916 on Seventh and Ash Streets.

EDWARD L. HARDY (1912–1913)

Hardy was born in Owasso, Michigan, in 1868. After earning degrees at the University of Michigan and University of Chicago, he came to California in 1899 to become the Assistant Headmaster of the Los Angeles Military Academy. He was Principal

of San Diego High School in 1906 before moving up the street to Twelfth and Park Boulevard as the President of San Diego Normal School. Dr. Hardy directed the college as it expanded from a two-year to a four-year liberal arts college. In 1931, he led the move of the school from University Heights to the outskirts of the city at Sixtieth Street. Dr. Hardy was President of San Diego State College from 1910 to 1935, when he retired as President Emeritus.

JOSEPH W. SEFTON JR.

ACTIVE IN THE EARLY GROWTH OF THE UNIVERSITY CLUB was San Diego banker Joseph W. Sefton Jr. The "dean of San Diego banking executives" was President and Board Chairman of San Diego Trust & Savings Bank until his retirement in 1962 after fifty-eight years at the bank.

Joseph W. Sefton Jr.
Courtesy of the 1909 University Club of San Diego Fine Arts Collection

Born in 1884 in Dayton, Ohio, Joseph Sefton Jr. came to San Diego in 1904 after attending Stanford University (as a footballer he played in the first Rose Bowl game in 1902). Joining his father, who had founded San Diego Trust in 1889, Sefton began his career as a bank messenger before rising to Vice-president in 1909. He became the bank's third President in 1935—a post he would hold until 1960.

Sefton was vitally engaged in many San Diego community organizations. He served for several years as President of the Society of Natural History and was the Public Relations Director for the Panama California Exposition in 1915. Sefton was a Director of the San Diego Chamber of Commerce, a San Diego Harbor Commissioner, and a life member of the Cuyamaca Club.

Joseph W. Sefton Jr. at the Panama California Exposition in 1915, photographed with John Barrett, President Taft's representative. *SDPL, Special Collections*

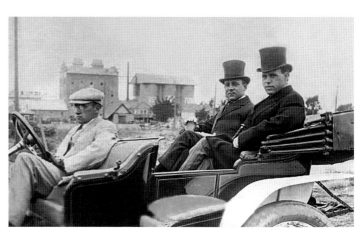

GORDON L. GRAY (1914)

Gray was the founder of San Diego's oldest law firm, known today as Gray, Cary, Ware & Freidenrich. Born in Barrien Springs, Michigan, in 1878, Gray was an honor student at Harvard, where he earned his law degree in 1903. He organized the first meeting of the San Diego Rotary Club in 1911. He organized the San Diego Museum Association and become a Director of the Merchants Association of San Diego. He was a founding member of the first Executive Committee of the Boy Scouts of America. In his later career, Gray was a Director of the San Diego Zoological Society for many years and was active until he died in 1967.

WILLIAM DOUGLAS (1915)

Real estate developer Douglas was known in San Diego as the promoter of Kensington Park—the first housing tract built in the Kensington-Talmadge development. As secretary of San Diego's "Chamber of Lands" and the selling agent for Kensington, Douglas supervised the grading of streets, the creation of sidewalks and curbs, and the selling of housing lots in a sixty-six-acre tract that opened in 1910.

DUNCAN MACKINNON (1916)

San Diego's respected Superintendent of Schools was born in Nova Scotia, Canada, in 1871. He earned his B.A. at Stanford University. He was hired as Principal of San Diego High School in 1905. He became the Superintendent of Schools the next year. MacKinnon's twelve-year tenure ended in controversy. He was popular among students and teachers, particularly after he supported a community drive to build a city arena near the high school—later known as Balboa Stadium. But many San Diegans considered the stadium a wasteful extravagance. Others disapproved because he was "a bachelor who lived at the University Club."

MacKinnon resigned as Superintendent in 1917 and became the President of the United States National Bank. In the last years of World War I, he served as the Food Administrator for San Diego City and County.

Portraits from 1918 to 1943 were photographed by Melvin H. Sykes and Elson-Alexandre of Los Angeles. *All Images courtesy of the 1909 University Club of San Diego Fine Arts Collection. Re-photographed by ZackBenson.com*

EDWARD L. HARDY (1912–1913)   GORDON L. GRAY (1914)   DUNCAN MACKINNON (1916)   A. H. SWEET (1917)

ADELBERT H. SWEET (1916–18)

A highly successful corporate lawyer and the County District Attorney, Sweet was born and raised in Ohio. He studied law at the University of Michigan before practicing law in Kansas. In 1885 he opened an office at Second and F Streets. As District Attorney from 1895 to 1898, Sweet successfully prosecuted several high-profile cases. Returning to corporate law after his term as D.A., he specialized in water and real estate issues. Sweet served as President of the County Bar Association, helped found San Diego's first Congregational Church, and donated time to the Masons, Elks, San Diego Country Club, Scholia Club, and the Tuesday Club. A. H. Sweet's home, designed by renowned architects Frank Mead and Richard Requa, is an architectural treasure. The 1914 home in Banker's Hill was designated a San Diego Historical Site in 1986.

CHARLES N. ANDREWS (1918)

Andrews, a distinguished judge, was raised in Minnesota before he came to San Diego in 1907. He practiced law for six years before his appointment as a Superior Court Judge by Governor Hiram Johnson, where he served for twenty-two years on the Superior Court, the longest continuous tenure in county history—often as the court's presiding Judge. He performed more marriages (and divorces) than any of Judge during his tenure. On October 3, 1917, Andrews made San Diego history when he seated the first female jurors in his courtroom, Miss F. A. Cooper and Mrs. Sarah T. Hale.

JOHN H. MCCORKLE (1919)

McCorkle, the former President of the San Diego County Bar Association, was born in Pennsylvania and graduated from the University of Michigan in 1892. Moving to Colorado, he practiced law in Pueblo for twenty-two years. McCorkle came to San Diego in 1914. He was also a Vice-president of the Chamber of Commerce, a member of the Cuyamaca Club, the Masons, and Knights of Pythias.

WILLET S. DORLAND (1920)

Dorland, a successful banker, was President of the Security Commercial and Savings Bank. Born in Salem, Iowa, in 1863, he attended Penn College, Iowa. Dorland took up banking in the 1890s in Texas before returning to Chicago. He came to San Diego in 1913 and advanced from the Cashier of the Security Commercial and Savings Bank to Bank President. During World War I, he was Chairman of the San Diego County Salvation Army War Fund, the Executive Committee of the Liberty Loan Committee, and Director of the local Red Cross and Boy Scouts. He was President of the Chamber of Commerce in 1917 and active in many civic organizations, including Knights of Pythias, Cuyamaca Club, Elks Club, and the San Diego Symphony.

MAYNARD C. HARDING (1921)

Born in Mason City in 1878. Dr. Harding practiced medicine in Ault, Colorado, until 1911. After postgraduate work in orthopedic surgery, he came to San Diego in 1913. Dr. Harding was a veteran of the Spanish-American War, and during World War I he worked as a surgeon in military hospitals. After the war, he joined the staff of Mercy Hospital where he practiced for nearly thirty years. He was a member of the College of Surgeons and the American Academy of Orthopedic Surgeons. Dorland was a founder and Board member of the San Diego Society for Crippled Children.

WILL H. MCFETRIDGE (1922)

McFetridge was born in 1871 in Baraboo, Wisconsin. A woolen manufacturer in San Diego, he helped found the San Diego Fine Arts Society.

Charles N. Andrews (1918)   John H. McCorkle (1919)   Ralph Bach (1924)   Charles M. Fox (1925)

Milton A. McRae (1926)   Jabez W. Fisher (1927)   Harrison G. Sloan (1928)   George H. Stone (1931)

Edward T. Guymon Jr. (1932)   Andrew J. Thornton (1933)   John M. Ward (1934)   Walter E. Walsh (1935)

Martin L. Ward (1923)

San Diego County District Attorney and State Senator Ward was born in Athens, Ohio, in 1850. A direct lineal descendent of John and Priscilla Alden, Ward was proud of his membership in the Mayflower Society. After graduation from Cornell College in Mount Vernon, Iowa, Ward wanted to go to law school but poverty led to a short teaching career instead. He was admitted to the Iowa Bar in 1876 and practiced law in Cedar Rapids until 1887, when he decided to move to San Diego where he settled in the new town of Chula Vista. He became the County District Attorney in 1892 and traveled to San Diego each workday in a horse-drawn buggy. He was elected to the California Senate in 1903 and served four years. After his Senate career, he practiced law with his two sons in the firm Ward, Ward, and Ward.

Ralph E. Bach (1924)

Insurance industry leader Bach moved from Montana in 1907 and attended San Diego High School. After graduating from Stanford University, Bach joined his father in the insurance business in 1917. The Bach Company merged in 1963 to become Cheverton-Bach. Bach served as Secretary-Treasurer of California Association of Insurance Agents and President of Independent Insurance Agents Association of California. He was a Director of San Diego Trust & Savings Bank and a Director of San Diego Gas & Electric Company.

Charles M. Fox (1925)

Fox, a practicing surgeon, was a graduate of Northwestern University Medical School and became an instructor there before becoming Attending Surgeon at St. Bernard's Hospital in Chicago. Dr. Fox came to San Diego in 1916 and served on the medical staffs of the County Hospital and Mercy Hospital. His wife Marie was the daughter of the renowned opera star Madame Ernestine Schumann-Heink. The Fox family lived for many years in her home at 9951 El Granito, regarded as the first house built on Grossmont Summit.

Milton A. McRae (1926)

McRae, a pioneer newspaperman and philanthropist, was born in Detroit in 1858. He took a temporary job as a reporter for the *Detroit Tribune* to pay his school bills and discovered his passion. At the *Cincinnati Post* in 1883, Colonel McRae (the title was strictly honorary) became friends with Managing Editor E. W. Scripps, where they formed the Scripps-McRae League of Newspapers, the first major chain of newspapers in the United States. McRae served on the Boards of the Scripps Memorial Hospital, Fine Arts Society, San Diego Historical Society, and Philharmonic Orchestra Society. Instrumental in founding the Boy Scouts of America, McRae was the third national President of the organization and the first President of the local Scouts. Before his death in 1930, Colonel McRae wrote a well-known book *Forty Years in Newspaperdom: The Autobiography of a Newspaper Man*.

Jabez W. Fisher (1927)

Fisher was a leader in San Diego civic affairs for forty-four years. He came to the city in 1911 after growing up in Massachusetts. He joined the Southwest Onyx and Marble Company in 1920 and became President in 1935—a position he held until his death September 1955. Fisher played an active role in the Civic Affairs Conference, a citizens group that helped reorganize San Diego's city government in 1932. He was also interested in water development, representing the region on the County Water Authority Board and the

Metropolitan Water District Board. Fisher was a past President of the San Diego Rowing Club, the Cornell University Association, and the San Diego Country Club. Fisher also served as a Director of the San Diego Natural History Museum.

HARRISON G. SLOAN (1928)

The distinguished attorney Sloan was the first native-born San Diegan to become University Club President. He was a founder of the San Diego County Bar Association and practiced law with Edgar Luce before forming his own law practice. His father, William A. Sloane, was a Justice on the California Supreme Court. Sloan attended the B Street School and Russ (San Diego) High School. At Pomona College, where he graduated in 1910 with Phi Beta Kappa honors, Sloane was a track star, winning the state championship in the 440-yard dash. He later coached the San Diego High School track team. Sloane was also an active member of the San Diego Yacht Club.

PAUL C. EDWARDS (1929)

Noted Scripps-Howard Newspaper Chain Executive Edwards was the Editor of the *San Diego Sun* from 1925 to 1932. Born in Knightstown, Indiana, in 1882, he moved to Palo Alto at the age of thirteen and graduated from Stanford University in 1906. He served as President of the Stanford Board of Trustees from 1948 to 1953. Edwards was a reporter for the *San Francisco Daily News* in 1907 and then became a founding Editor of the *Houston Press*. He returned to California in 1925 as the Editor of the *San Diego Sun*. After seven years, Edwards rejoined the *Daily News*, as Managing Editor. In San Diego, Edwards was a Director of the Chamber of Commerce, a Trustee of the local YMCA, a Director of the Rotary Club, and President of the University Club in 1929. At

the time of his death at age eighty, Edwards was a nationally recognized newsman. President Herbert Hoover eulogized Edwards as "an outstanding editor. . . . He served the American people in scores of directions with great devotion and his passing is a loss to us all."

ADDISON E. ELLIOTT (1930)

Elliot, a noted x-ray specialist, was born in Table Grove, Illinois, in 1876. After schooling at Knox College in Galesburg and Rush Medical College in Chicago, he spent two years in Vienna, Austria, in postgraduate study. He spent ten years in El Centro and then moved to San Diego in 1925. He joined Dr. Lyell C. Kinney in an x-ray laboratory practice that continued until his death in 1934. Besides his association with the University Club, Dr. Elliott was a member of the American College of Physicians and the American Roentgenological Society.

GEORGE H. STONE (1931)

Prominent attorney Stone was born in South Dakota in 1883, and studied law at the University of Minnesota. He came to San Diego in 1915 and began a thirty-year law partnership with attorney Glen H. Munkelt in 1921. Stone was once head of the Community Chest (precursor to the United Way) and was a strong supporter of the local YMCA. As the Secretary of the San Diego Hospital Association, Stone was a tireless advocate for a new community hospital for San Diego. His work would lead to the opening of the Sharp Memorial Hospital, built on Linda Vista mesa after his death.

EDWARD T. GUYMON JR. (1932)

Guymon, a prominent financier in San Diego and perhaps America's most celebrated collector of mystery books. Born in Kansas in 1900, Guymon came to California with his family and attended

Occidental College in Los Angeles. After graduation in 1922, he came to San Diego and began
buying real estate in downtown San Diego.

Guymon was a founding member of San Diegans
Inc., a group of property owners that promoted
downtown development and led the campaign
to build the City Hall-Civic Center Complex on C
Street. Guymon also built San Diego's first multilevel parking garage at Seventh Avenue and C
Street. He was very interested in local history and
restored the historic Pendleton House in Old Town
in 1937.

He began accumulating first-edition mystery
books in the 1930s. In the next fifty years, his
growing collection of books, manuscripts, pho-
tographs, and film scripts became nationally
known. The Ned Guymon Mystery and Detective
Fiction Collection (sixteen thousand volumes) was
donated to Occidental College before Guymon's
death in 1983.

ANDREW J. THORNTON (1933)

Thornton was a San Diego physician who was
born in Iowa in 1882. He came to San Diego in
1910. Dr. Thornton was an active member of the
San Diego County Medical Society and served as
President in 1924.

Dr. Thornton was a well-known pediatrician and
the Medical Director of the San Diego Rest Haven
Preventorium, a renowned tuberculosis hospital
for children. In 1935, he was appointed by the
Wisconsin Alumni Research Foundation to super-
vise an intensive study of nutritional diseases in
children. Working with the San Diego Department
of Health, Dr. Thornton made clinical observations
of large numbers of San Diego children.

JOHN M. WARD (1934)

Ward was born in Cedar Rapids, Iowa, in 1883,
but his family came west and settled in Chula Vista.
His father, Martin L. Ward, became a California
State Senator. Ward graduated from San Diego
High School and Stanford University before attending Harvard Law School. He received his law
degree from Stanford in 1909 and was admitted to
the California Bar the same year.

Specializing in corporate and trust law, Ward
represented many prominent San Diegans and
was the executor of many large estates. He was
a member of the Cuyamaca Club, Rowing Club,
Elks Club, Fine Arts Society, San Diego Historical
Society, San Diego Yacht Club, and the Society of
Mayflower Descendants.

WALTER E. WALSH (1935)

Walsh, a former President of the San Diego County
Dental Association, was born in Ottawa, Kansas,
in 1872. He moved east in his twenties and graduated from the Philadelphia Dental College in 1900.
Walsh became active in his profession, becoming President of the local Dental Association. He
was a life member of the San Diego Elks Lodge,
and was particularly interested in the work of the
Neighborhood House, a "social settlement" organization. Dr. Walsh died in March 1949.

RAYMOND M. WANSLEY (1936)

A San Diego City Councilman, Wansley was
born in Texas in 1908. He graduated from San
Diego High School and Pomona College when he
became a public accountant. Two decades later
he decided to study law at the former Balboa Law
College in San Diego. He joined the California
Bar in 1947 and eventually practiced with his own
firm, Torrance & Wansley. Wansley was active

RAYMOND M. WANSLEY (1936)

CHESTER O. TANNER (1937)

RAMEL K. SYBERT, (1938)

FRED KUNZEL (1939)

CLINTON G. ABBOTT (1940)

FRED G. JACKSON (1941)

RENWICK THOMPSON (1942)

LESLIE H. REDELINGS (1943)

HARRY G. MALM (1944)

EDGAR A. LUCE (1945)

LORENZ F. DE JULIEN (1946)

HALL HOLDER (1947)

with the San Diego Chamber of Commerce, a member of the Cuyamaca Club, and President of the Community Chest. He served on the San Diego City Council from 1935 to 1939, where he was noted for his frequent verbal battles with San Diego Mayor Percy J. Benbough.

CHESTER O. TANNER (1937)

Tanner graduated from the University of Minnesota, School of Medicine in 1917 and joined the Navy Medical Corps at the end of World War I. He served as a surgeon aboard the USS *Wadsworth*, flagship of the first U.S. destroyer squadron sent overseas. He transferred to the Naval Hospital in San Diego in 1919 and joined the staff at St. Joseph's Hospital (later Mercy Hospital) and remained there until retirement in 1957. He was also on the staff of the San Diego County Hospital (now UCSD Medical Center) for twenty-five years, the last years as Chief of Surgery. A member of the American College of Surgeons, Dr. Tanner was President of the San Diego County Medical Society, served on the County Grand Jury, and was a member of the San Diego Board of Health. He died in 1984 at the age of ninety-two.

RAMEL K. SYBERT (1938)

Businessman Sybert was born in Bellingham, Washington, in 1896. He attended the San Diego Army and Navy Academy in Pacific Beach and graduated from San Diego High School.

After serving in the Army in World War I, Sybert worked as a bookkeeper for a local meat packer. He later owned an auto service station, an upholstery store, and then worked as a tire salesman. By 1930 he was an executive with Hage's Ltd., a San Diego dairy and ice cream company. Sybert worked for Hage's for twenty-five years and

remained on the job for seven more years after Hage's was sold to Foremost Foods in 1954. Sybert served on the County Grand Jury and was a life member of the San Diego Rowing Club. In 1936 he was elected a Director of the National Association of Credit Men, the first San Diegan so honored. He died on January 23, 1976.

FRED KUNZEL (1939)

U.S. District Court Judge Kunzel served two years as an Army Private in World War I before attending Stanford University. After earning his J.D. degree from Stanford in 1927, he quickly advanced to partner in the law firm of Luce, Forward, Kunzel and Scripps. Kunzel rejoined the military in 1942 and retired after World War II as a Commander. He specialized in corporate and admiralty law. President Dwight Eisenhower appointed Kunzel to the U.S. District Court for the Southern District of California in 1959. As a Federal Judge, Kunzel strongly advocated a separate court district for San Diego-Imperial instead of being a subdistrict of the Los Angeles-based court. Change finally came in 1966, three years before Kunzel's death.

CLINTON G. ABBOTT (1940)

A well-known scientist Abbott was Director of the San Diego Natural History Museum from 1922 until his death in 1946. The author of scores of articles on animals and birds, Abbott built the collections of the museum in Balboa Park until it became a nationally recognized institution.

Born of American parents in Liverpool, England, in 1861, he earned a degree from Columbia University in 1903 and attended Cornell in 1914–15. He became Secretary and Editor of the New York State Conservation Commission from 1918 to

1921. Inheriting the ownership of an eastern steel business, he managed the firm against his will for ten years. After doctors advised him to relocate to a less severe climate, he chose San Diego, and became Director of the Natural History Museum. In his later years, Abbott became an avid photographer, participated in the restoration of Old Town San Diego, and led a Chamber of Commerce committee to advise on the re-creation of the original Spanish-Mexican architecture of the early pueblo.

FREDERICK G. JACKSON (1941)

A noted art patron and prominent in San Diego civic and cultural affairs Jackson was born in 1881 in Prides Crossing, Massachusetts. He earned a master's degree in chemistry at Harvard in 1905. After leaving the university, Jackson studied American Indian ceramics, and developed an interest in art that would last his lifetime. Jackson served in World War I as a Navy Lieutenant and during World War II he served as a member of the San Diego Draft Board. He joined San Diego's Fine Arts Society in 1933 and was later elected to the Board. He was Treasurer of the organization in 1937 and President from 1945 to 1947. Jackson was an avid stamp collector, who inherited his parents' collection that was started in 1860. He later donated the collection to the Fine Arts Gallery. Jackson was also an advisor to the Children's Home in San Diego, and was active with the San Diego Floral Association.

RENWICK THOMPSON SR. (1942)

A former President of the San Diego County Bar Association and an attorney in San Diego for forty-eight years, Thompson was born in British Columbia and came to San Diego in his mid-teens. President of his graduating class at San Diego High School in 1916, he graduated from the University

of Southern California Law School. He joined his father, Adam Thompson, to form the law firm of Thompson & Thompson in 1919. Interested in amateur sports, Thompson was a local Commissioner for the American Athletic Union (AAU) and many other athletic organizations in the 1940s.

LESLIE H. REDELINGS (1943)

Redelings was born in Marinette, Wisconsin, and attended medical school at Johns Hopkins University. From 1915 to 1981, Dr. Redelings was a Fellow in Surgery at the famed Mayo Clinic in Rochester, Minnesota. He joined the staff of Mercy Hospital in 1920 and was President of the San Diego County Medical Society in 1931 and President of the San Diego Academy of Medicine in 1937. He was active in many San Diego civic organizations including the Museum of Man, the Historical Society, the Floral Association, and the Museum of Natural History.

HARRY G. MALM (1944)

Nebraska-born Malm came to San Diego in 1927, after earning a law degree from the University of Colorado. In San Diego, Malm pursued a business career, eventually becoming Senior Vice-president of John Burnham & Company. Malm served as President of many local organizations, including the San Diego Consular Corps, the Kiwanis Club, the Children's Health Center, the Union Club, and the San Diego Society for Crippled Children. Malm served as the Vice Consul of Sweden from 1956 until his death in 1973. In 1965, he was made a Knight of the Royal Order of Vasa by King Gustav V of Sweden.

EDGAR A. LUCE SR. (1945)

Luce was the son of Moses A. Luce, the founder of the prominent law firm known today as Luce,

Forward, Hamilton & Scripps. Edgar Luce was born in San Diego in 1881. After graduating from Stanford University in 1905 he joined a friend in the gold fields of Calaveras County. After six months, the discouraged gold seeker read for the California Bar (bypassing law school) and joined his father's law firm in 1906. Six years later he was elected a State senator. He resigned that office in 1918 to join the Army Air Corps. After World War I Luce was appointed to the Superior Court and later was elected to a four-year term. Judge Luce left the court to join Phil D. Swing in private practice. Swing was a former Superior Court judge for Imperial County and a future U.S. Congressman.

Judge Luce was always interested in politics. A Progressive in the Republican Party, he attended the 1912 Republican Convention in Chicago, where former President Theodore Roosevelt bolted the party to form the Bull Moose Party and run against incumbent William Howard Taft. Fifty years later Luce would lead the Citizens for Eisenhower organization.

Lorenz F. DeJulien (1946)

Born in 1899, DeJulien was a college professor with a distinguished teaching career at San Diego State. Before entering education, DeJulien was the Head of Merchandise for San Diego's famed Marston Store. He was also a real estate broker, and for a time owned a women's sportswear store in Hillcrest. In his eighteen-year career at San Diego State, he taught business classes, retiring as Professor Emeritus of business administration.

Hall G. Holder Sr. (1947)

Holder, born in Lansing, Michigan, earned his medical degree at Cornell University and served his residency at Bellevue in New York City. During World War II, Dr. Holder served in the U.S. Army Medical Corps, rising to the rank of Colonel. Working at San Diego's Camp Callan in 1942, he was credited with improvements in the composition of sulfa drugs—important antibiotics used before the introduction of penicillin. Dr. Holder worked for twenty-five years at the San Diego County Hospital, retiring in 1952 as the Chief of Surgery. He was also a past President of the County Medical Society. Dr. Holder would die tragically in an automobile accident in 1976. A double-amputee, he used hand controls for his car, which malfunctioned, plunging his car off a cliff after attending a family wedding in Santa Clara County.

Howard F. Taylor (1948)

Taylor was born in Indiana in 1899. An Army veteran of World War I, Taylor was a car dealer in San Diego for thirty-three years. He founded his own company—the Taylor Motor Company, later Howard Taylor Dodge. Taylor was a past President of the San Diego County Automobile Dealers Association. He was also a President of the San Diego County Grand Jury.

Orlan K. Bullard (1949)

An internationally known oral surgeon, Bullard came to San Diego in 1908 where he grew up in the Golden Hill area and graduated from Russ High School, later known as San Diego High. Just out of school, he worked at the Panama-California Exposition as the Secretary to the Pinkerton Detective Agency. After World War I, where he served in the Navy as a radio electrician, Bullard graduated from the USC School of Dentistry in 1921. He began his dental practice in San Diego. Dr. Bullard studied dental surgery in St. Louis in 1927, and returning to San Diego, he began building a national reputation for oral surgery.

Howard F. Taylor (1948)

Orlan K. Bullard (1949)

Harold G. Smith (1950)

Edward S. Hope (1951)

Baylor Brooks (1952)

Werner W. Duemling (1953)

Joseph F. Sinnott (1954)

Kary Canatsey (1955)

Jack M. Harrison (1957)

Edgar A. Luce Jr. (1958)

Jon R. Robson (1959)

Allan S. Klauber (1960)

He was a founder of the American Board of Oral Surgeons, a Fellow of the American College of Dentists, and President of San Diego County Dental Society. At the time of his death at age ninety-four, he was still an active member of community organizations such as the Rotary Club, San Diego and Mission Valley Country Clubs, and the San Diego Zoological Society.

HAROLD G. SMITH (1950)

The founder of the H. G. Lumber Company, Smith was a native of Union, Oregon. He graduated from Sweetwater High School and attended the University of California, Berkeley. Smith started his lumber company in 1934. He joined the University Club the next year. He was also a member and past President of the Cuyamaca Club, and a Trustee of the Point Loma Community Presbyterian Church.

EDWARD S. HOPE (1951)

Hope was an investment broker and civic leader. He graduated from San Diego High School and attended San Diego State but never graduated. He supplemented his education throughout his life by voracious reading of nonfiction in many subject areas. At age twenty-one, Hope joined the Bond Department of Southern Trust & Savings and began his career in investments. Six years later—in the midst of the Great Depression—Hope formed the E. S. Hope Company, specializing in stocks and government bonds. In 1955, with his brokerage company one of the largest in San Diego, he built his own office building at Fourth Avenue and Laurel Street. His company merged with New York-based Eastman Dillon.

Hope was an active Republican who once ran for Congress. Withdrawing before the primary election he served for many years on the County Central

Committee. He was President of Francis W. Parker School, the San Diego chapter of the American Cancer Society, the Children's Hospital, and the San Diego Society for Crippled Children. Besides his lifelong interest in books, Hope was an avid sailor, and enjoyed astronomy and gardening.

BAYLOR "SKIP" BROOKS (1952)

A pioneering educator at San Diego State College, Geology Professor Brooks was born in Des Moines, Iowa, in 1906. After graduating from Stanford University, Baylor attended graduate school at Oxford University in England, Harvard University, and the University of Iowa. He joined the faculty of San Diego State Teachers College (precursor to SDSU) in 1931, the same year the campus moved from University Heights to Montezuma Mesa. At the time, the subject of geology was only offered as an elective. Under his guidance the curriculum grew, becoming the Department of Geological Sciences—now one of the ten largest geology programs in the country. He was a former President of the San Diego Society of Natural History. He lived in Kensington in the 1950s, moving to Poway after his retirement in 1966.

WERNER W. DUEMLING (1953)

Duemling earned his medical degree from the University of Michigan. World War II brought him to San Diego where he was Chief of Dermatology Service at the Naval Hospital until retiring from the Navy in 1946 and going into private practice. In 1963, Duemling was appointed the honorary West German Consul in San Diego. He noted the appointment "recognized the increasing importance of San Diego in world trade." He was awarded the Order for Meritorious Service from the Federal Republic of Germany in 1970. Dr. Duemling served on the medical staffs of Mercy,

Sharp, and Grossmont Hospitals. He was a past President of the San Diego Dermatological Society and of the San Diego chapter of the American Cancer Society.

JOSEPH F. SINNOTT (1954)

The respected Chief Executive of the San Diego Gas & Electric Company, Sinnott was a native of Philadelphia, but had strong ties to San Diego. His mother, Mary Henrietta Luce, was a member of the pioneer Luce family. After earning a degree in electrical engineering from Harvard University in 1929, he began working for San Diego Gas & Electric as a meter tester. He became Engineering Vice-president in 1962. The next year, he became Company President and Chief Executive Officer. Sinnott would lead the utility company in a period of rapid growth; he would estimate that electrical power provided by SDG&E had multiplied twenty times by the time he retired in 1971.

Sinnott served on the Boards of several local organizations including the Sharp Memorial Hospital, the Natural History Museum, and the Zoological Society. He was a President of San Diegans Inc. in 1969, and headed the State Highway Commission for two years after his appointment by Governor Ronald Reagan.

KARY CANATSEY (1955)

Born in Kansas in 1904, Canatsey ran an electrical manufacturing firm in Kansas City. He came to La Jolla in 1945 for a summer vacation and "fell in love with this delightful place." And returned to La Jolla to live. In retirement Canatsey served as Chairman of the La Jolla Community Chest, and in 1951 he was elected President of the Scripps Memorial Hospital. He remained active in community philanthropy until his death in 1986.

FRANK L. HOPE (1956)

Revered architect Hope was the son of a freight agent for the Santa Fe Railway, who came to San Diego from Los Angeles with his family in 1912. After briefly attending San Diego High School, he left school to work in the shipyards during World War I. He attended the University of California, Berkeley. Hope founded his architectural and engineering firm in 1928. The company's landmark structures included the original buildings of Children's Hospital in Kearny Mesa in 1954, the eighteen-story Home Tower (San Diego's first high-rise building) in 1963, the blue-domed Immaculata at the University of San Diego in 1964, and San Diego Stadium—now Qualcomm, in 1967. Hope was a Director of the San Diego Chamber of Commerce, President of the Planning Commission, and Director of Home Federal Bank. He belonged to the San Diego Rowing Club and the San Diego Navy League. Hope was a familiar figure at the San Diego Yacht Club, hosting gin rummy games among friends aboard his forty-two-foot boat, *High Hopes*.

JACK M. HARRISON (1957)

Attorney Harrison was a native of Texas who attended the California Western School of Law in San Diego and was admitted to the State Bar in 1947. Tax law was Harrison's specialty; he was a member of the California Society of Public Accountants. He practiced in San Diego as a partner in the law firm of Harrison and Watson.

EDGAR A. LUCE JR. (1958)

Born in 1924, Edgar A. Luce Jr. was the grandson of San Diego pioneer attorney Moses A. Luce and the brother of banker Gordon Luce. He attended San Diego High School, where he excelled in track and field, and edited the school newspaper. Luce earned his law degree from Stanford University in 1948 and joined the San Diego law firm of Luce Forward Hamilton & Scripps, the firm his grandfather had founded in 1873. Specializing in commercial litigation, Luce became of partner in 1955 and managing partner in 1978.

Luce served on the Board of the San Diego Center for Children, and offering pro bono legal help to the Junior League, the Wednesday Club, and the San Diego Symphony. He maintained an interest in sports throughout his life, coaching Little League and raising money for the San Diego Senior Olympics. In his sixties, Luce competed in the Senior Olympics in tennis and the high jump. After retiring in 1996, he maintained his office and worked as a mentor to young attorneys.

JON R. ROBSON (1959)

At age thirty-two, Robson was the youngest President of the University Club. Born in Seattle in 1927, Robson attended schools in Los Angeles and graduated from UCLA in 1949. He began a forty-year career in the insurance industry when he joined the Bach Company in San Diego. Robson formed his own company: Robson, Cavignac, and Associates. He was President of the San Diego Lion's Club and the Executive's Association of San Diego. He was a jazz aficionado and a sports fan. An active member of the San Diego Yacht Club, Robson often raced competitively. At the time of his death in 2001, he enjoyed sailing a thirty-six-foot clipper-rigged Cheoy Lee called *The Dragon Lady*.

ALLAN S. KLAUBER (1960)

Klauber was a native-born San Diegan from a pioneer family who graduated from San Diego High School and Stanford University. He began working for the family business—the Klauber Wangenheim

Company—in 1927. He served as President of the wholesale grocery firm from 1935 to 1965, when he became Chairman of the Board. Klauber was Director of the Western Metal Supply Company and the Southern Title Company. He was President of the Community Chest (United Way), the San Diego Employers Association, and Francis W. Parker School. Klauber was also a Director of the Chamber of Commerce, the Convention and Visitors Bureau, the Door of Hope, and the local chapters of the American Red Cross and the American Cancer Society.

GEORGE R. SAUNDERS (1961)

San Diego native Saunders attended San Diego State College before graduating from the California Institute of Technology in 1944. Commissioned as a Lieutenant in the last year of World War II, Saunders served as a Naval engineer.

Saunders began his career as a design engineer with the City of San Diego Water Department, working on the Sutherland Dam and the Alvarado Water Filtration Plant at Lake Murray. As a construction engineer in the 1950s, he worked on the rapid expansion of the San Diego city schools. Saunders started his own structural engineering firm in 1958 and worked on the San Diego Museum of Art, Sea World, UCSD, the Community College District, the Eleventh Naval District, and the Unified Port District.

Strongly interested in historical structures, he used his engineering expertise in the preservation of the Stewart House in Old Town, the Villa Montezuma in Golden Hill, the Hotel del Coronado, and buildings in the Gaslamp Quarter. Saunders' many civic group memberships included the San Diego Historical Society, the Children's Hospital, and the San Diego Historical Sites Board.

George Saunders (1961)

Eugene L. Freeland Jr. (1962)

Leonard H. Storay (1963)

Gordon C. Luce (1964)

Maurice T. Watson (1965)

J. Frederick Conrad (1966)

W. Daniel Larsen (1967)

Vance A. Gustafson (1968)

Hodge N. Crabtree (1969)

Jere H. Lien (1970)

Oscar F. Irwin (1971)

Edward T. Simms Jr. (1972)

EUGENE L. FREELAND JR. (1962)

San Diego native Freeland was a noted attorney who practiced with Gray, Cary, Ames & Frye from 1954 to 1988. Born in 1925, he grew up in Mission Hills, attended Pomona College and UCLA, and earned his law degree from UC Hastings College of the Law. Freeland began practicing law with Ralph Waverly Wallace. A few years later he joined Gray Cary. He was the firm's first divorce lawyer but he specialized in civil litigation, particularly the field of eminent domain. Freeland was active in the Rancho Santa Fe Community Center and Ducks Unlimited. He was also an avid cook who won blue ribbons at the Del Mar Fair, and collected glasswork from Tiffany and Steuben.

LEONARD H. STORAY (1963)

Storay was born in New York in 1912. Storay came to San Diego in the 1930s and found work with the County Department of Public Welfare as a social worker. He was a veteran of World War II, enlisting as a Private in December 1942. Two years later, as a First Lieutenant, Storay would win the Bronze Star for heroism in action near Elsenborn, Belgium, in the Battle of the Bulge. After the war, Storay returned to San Diego and worked for many years for California Credit System.

GORDON C. LUCE (1964)

Luce, the third-generation San Diegan, was born in 1925. He attended San Diego High School and edited the school newspaper, *The Russ*. Out of high school as World War II began, Luce joined the Army and won a Bronze Star as an infantryman in General George S. Patton's Third Army.

After the war, Luce earned a master's degree in business administration at Stanford University in 1952. Two years later he began his banking career, working for Home Federal Savings—rising to Senior Vice-president by 1963. Luce ran Ronald Reagan's successful gubernatorial campaign in San Diego in 1966 and joined the Governor in Sacramento as the California Secretary of Business and Transportation.

Luce returned to San Diego and banking in 1969, joining San Diego Federal Savings. By 1978, San Diego Federal was the most profitable savings and loan in the nation. It became Great American Savings Bank in 1983 and Luce would run the company until his retirement in 1991.

Luce supported San Diego downtown development, promoting urban renewal and joining several cultural organizations. He was President of San Diegans Inc. in 1970, and in the 1980s he was President of the San Diego Museum of Art and Chairman of the Scripps Clinic and Research Foundation Board of Trustees.

MAURICE T. WATSON (1965)

The son of recent English immigrants, first-generation San Diegan Watson was born in 1925. After graduation from Stanford University, he was admitted to the California Bar in 1956 and soon joined the firm of Torrance and Wansley. Six years later he partnered with Jack M. Harrison, in the firm Harrison and Watson. Watson served as President of the San Diego County Bar Association in 1975. He was an active member of the Point Loma Association and San Diego Rotary, and a contributor to the Mercy Hospital Foundation and the Quail Botanical Gardens.

J. FREDERICK CONRAD (1966)

San Diego orthodontist Conrad moved to San Diego in 1926. After attending San Diego High School and San Diego State College, Conrad studied dentistry at the University of California Medical Center in San Francisco. He graduated in 1938. During World War II, Dr. Conrad served as a Dental Officer on the USS *Altair* in the Philippines and later at the Naval Training Center in San Diego. Resuming his San Diego practice after the war, he was a member of the San Diego County Dental Society. He retired in 1989, however along with his wife Margaret, Dr. Conrad continued his involvement in many civic groups including the San Diego Crippled Children's Society, the San Diego Yacht Club, the San Diego Aerospace Museum, and the Committee of 100.

W. DANIEL LARSEN (1967)

Born in 1928, Larsen is the son of a building contractor from Denmark, who immigrated to the United States in 1909. His father, Ben O. Larsen, built the Ford Building in Balboa Park. After graduation from UC Berkeley in 1951, W. Daniel Larsen followed his father's footsteps in San Diego. Larsen was the President of the San Diego chapter of Associated General Contractors. In 1968, Governor Ronald Reagan appointed him to the State Contractors License Board, where he served two four-year terms. He also served as a Port Commissioner. Larsen was President of San Diego Consular Corps and became the Honorary Danish Consul in San Diego in 1964, a position he held for the next thirty-four years. The consular position was inherited from his father, who served as Consul from 1950 to 1963.

VANCE A. GUSTAFSON (1968)

Born in San Diego in 1931, securities dealer Gustafson was President of Gustafson Financial Inc. Gustafson is a San Diego Rotary member and very active with the San Diego Yacht Club. An experienced sailor, Gustafson owns and races the eighty-year-old yacht *Jade*, which was once owned by locally famed yachtsman Joseph Jessop.

HODGE N. CRABTREE (1969)

Crabtree graduated from San Diego High School and earned his B.A. degree from Occidental College. After serving as a Navy Lieutenant in World War II, Crabtree attended medical school at the University of Michigan before returning to San Diego to begin his professional career in 1953.

He became Chief of Surgery at Mercy Hospital and the Chief of Staff at University Hospital. He was also a Counselor at the San Diego County Medical Society and a Director of the San Diego Blood Bank. His community interests included the Rest and Aspiration Society of San Diego, Ducks Unlimited, and the Audubon Society. Dr. Crabtree died in an automobile accident in 1975, when his car left the road below Mexicali as he drove to join friends for a fishing expedition in San Felipe.

JERE H. LIEN (1970)

Born in Illinois in 1932, Lien was an industrialist—the Vice-president of the Lien Chemical Company in Escondido. The Lien family owns and lives in the famed "Woreland Castle," built in Valley Center by the writer and artist Isaac Frazee in 1893. Jere Lien died in Valley Center in 1995.

OSCAR F. IRWIN (1971)

Irwin, a San Diego native, graduated from Hoover High School and San Diego State College, before serving in the U.S. Army from 1945 to 1947. Irwin attended Stanford University Law School where he was the Managing Editor of the *Stanford Law Review*. After graduation in 1954, he formed a successful partnership with attorney William Hillyer. Their firm, Hillyer and Irwin, grew to forty lawyers by 1993. He specialized in construction law and he represented San Diego construction companies, architects, engineers, and public agencies. He was elected a Fellow of the American Bar Association in 1983. Irwin was on the Board of Directors of the San Diego Taxpayer's Association and a member of the President's Circle at San Diego State University. He served on the Citizen's Advisory Committee for Racial Integration for the San Diego Unified School District. The committee studied voluntary means of achieving integration in local schools through magnet schools.

EDWARD T. SIMMS JR. (1972)

Simms was a banker and the Vice-president of the Real Estate and Loan Departments of San Diego Trust & Savings Bank. A native of Dallas, Texas, Simms graduated from the University of Texas, but also attended Rice and Baylor Universities. In World War II, he served as an Army Air Force test pilot. He began his career at San Diego Trust in mortgage banking in 1962 and was instrumental in making loans that led to the development Rancho Bernardo and the Golden Triangle.

WILL HIPPEN JR. (1973–74)

U.S. diplomat and businessman Will Hippen Jr. graduated from the Merchant Marine Academy and the Foreign Service from Georgetown University in 1947. He went to work for the U.S.

State Department and in 1951 he moved to San Diego to begin a new career in the aircraft and insurance businesses. He traveled in the Orient and became an Asian art expert. In the 1960s he authored a column on the subject for the *San Diego Union*. He represented San Diego in 1957 in the San Diego Yokohama Friendship Commission. Ten years later the commission became the San Diego–Yokohama Sister City Society with Hippen as the founding President. In 1975 he was named the first Honorary Consul General of Japan. Will Hippen died in February 1988.

HOWARD B. LEVINSON (1975)

Community banker Levenson has been Chairman and Chief Executive of Western Financial Corporation since 1976. Levenson graduated from San Diego State College with a degree in business administration. Since the mid-1960s, he held numerous managerial positions in the securities industry. Levenson has been a Director of many publicly traded companies. As a banker, he served on the Board of Directors of Southwest Bancorp, Southwest Bank, and Southwest Thrift and Loan. Levenson is also a prior Chairman of the Board of Governors of the Grossmont Hospital Foundation. In 2008, Levenson was instrumental in the formation of Vibra Bank, the only bi-cultural, Latino bank in San Diego County. He now serves on the Board of Directors of Vibra, which is based in Chula Vista.

GEORGE S. DELAFIELD (1976)

Delafield has been a practicing attorney since 1961. Born in New Jersey, Delafield graduated from Amherst College in Massachusetts. He earned his law degree from Harvard University. Delafield is an avid genealogist and is active with the Delafield Family Association, founded in 1912. The

WILL HIPPEN JR. (1973–74)

HOWARD B. LEVENSON (1975)

GEORGE S. DELAFIELD (1976)

ROBERT E. FISCHER (1977)

ROY E. ERWIN (1978)

ALAN B. LORD (1979)

STEPHEN P. OGGEL (1980)

LOUIS L. GARDAY (1981)

VINCENT E. BENSTEAD (1982)

PHILIP L. GILDRED JR. (1983)

WILLIAM C. HISCOCK (1984)

MICHAEL B. BIXLER (1985–86)

Association collects and preserves the history of its family, which descends from John Delafield, who immigrated to New York from England in 1783.

ROBERT E. FISCHER (1977)

Fischer, a CPA and partner in Arthur Young and Company, was an officer in the San Diego chapter of the National Conference of Christians and Jews and served as the Board Chairman in 1983.

ROY E. ERWIN (1978)

Insurance executive Erwin attended UCLA. Before graduation he joined the Navy and served in the Pacific in World War II. After the war, he joined the John Burnham Company where he would work for the next thirty-five years. Head of the Insurance Department he rose to Executive Vice-president and Chief Operating Officer. After retiring in 1982, Erwin founded two insurance companies: Beech Street Insurance Services and Magna Carta Insurance Ltd. He served on the Boards of the Children's Hospital, the Lemon Grove chapter of the Red Cross, and the Helen Woodward Animal Center in Rancho Santa Fe. Erwin lived for many years in the Mount Helix-La Mesa area but moved to Del Mar in the late 1980s, where he died in June 1991.

ALAN B. LORD (1979)

Banker Lord was the Executive Vice-president of the Bank of San Diego. In 1979, Lord served as Chairman of "America's Finest City" festivities. He was elected President of the California chapter of the American Banking Institute in 1986.

STEPHEN P. OGGEL (1980)

Attorney Oggel was born in Monmouth, Illinois, in 1942. After undergraduate study at Vanderbilt University, he earned a law degree at George Washington University in Washington, D.C. Oggel followed law school with three years as a Captain in the U.S. Marine Corps. Oggel practices real estate and business litigation. He teaches legal studies and has lectured at the University of California at San Diego, the Oasis Learning Institute, the American Management Association, and, since 2005, the Thomas Jefferson School of Law.

LOUIS J. GARDAY (1981)

Financial planner and investment banker Garday was elected President at age thirty-five. He earned a B.A. in business and accounting from California State University, Los Angeles, in 1968. After graduation, he worked for Arthur Young & Company. In 1973, Garday began working for the John Burnham Company, where he rose to Chief Financial Officer and eventually, President. After thirteen years at Burnham, Garday founded the highly successful real estate investment trust, Burnham Pacific Properties. Garday left San Diego in 1994 to found and manage Carolina Capital Markets, a REIT consulting firm in Columbia, South Carolina. He later moved to Denver and headed the Certified Financial Planner Board of Standards. Most recently, Louis Garday has been the Hedge Fund Director at Carrington Capital Markets in Greenwich, Connecticut.

VINCENT E. BENSTEAD (1982)

Benstead was born in Los Angeles County but spent his professional career in San Diego, working thirty-nine years with Price Waterhouse Coopers, where he audited major San Diego banks: San Diego Trust & Savings, La Jolla Bank and Trust, Scripps Bank, and First National Bank. Benstead founded Legacy Bank, which merged with Landmark National Bank in 2005, where he served as Vice-chairman. He has served on the Boards of the Scripps Research Institute, the San Diego Aircraft Carrier Museum, the Scripps Memorial Hospital Foundation, and the Greater San Diego Sports Association. He is a past President of the Holiday Bowl, and active with the Desert Pacific Boy Scouts, the San Diego Civic Light Opera, and the San Diego Multiple Sclerosis Society.

Philip L. Gildred Jr. (1983)

Gildred, the son of civic leader Philip L. Gildred Sr.—who was once honored as "Mr. San Diego"—was born in 1936 and grew up in San Diego. After college, Gildred went to work for his family's businesses, where he has been a Director and President of the Gildred Companies and the Secretary-Treasurer of the Gildred Building Company. He has also been a Director for Burnham Pacific Properties. Gildred was a founder and Director at the Sharp Hospital Foundation, a founder and President of the San Diego Automotive Museum in Balboa Park, and a longtime Board member of the San Diego Historical Society. Gildred was also instrumental in the revitalization of the San Diego Symphony, which moved into the renovated Fox Theater—originally developed by the Gildred family—in 1986.

William C. Hiscock (1984)

Attorney Hiscock earned his law degree from the University of Michigan Law School following service in the infantry in World War II. He came to California in 1951 and started practicing law in Los Angeles. After twenty years, Hiscock moved to Coronado and opened his office in downtown San Diego. Still an active attorney in his eighties, his law firm—now based in Coronado--specializes in estate planning. While Hiscock continues to enjoy legal work, he is also an avid lawn bowler and an active member of the Coronado and San Diego Lawn Bowling Clubs. In 2012, he was inducted into the United States Lawn Bowls Association Hall of Fame.

Michael B. Bixler (1985–86)

Bixler, a former Lieutenant Commander and Aviator served tours aboard USS *Bennington* and USS *Kitty Hawk*, earned a master of science degree at the Naval Postgraduate School in Monterey in 1971. Bixler graduated from the University of California, Berkeley, with a bachelor's degree from the College of Letters and Science, on a NROTC scholarship. In 1977, Bixler was made Vice-president within the Global Private Client Group at Merrill Lynch. As a past Club President, Bixler was part of the successful effort to move the Club membership to Symphony Towers.

A two-term Mayor of Imperial Beach, Bixler encouraged a partnership with the Port District in redeveloping the long-neglected beachfront. He led the development of Portwood Pier Plaza, Palm Avenue Street-End Overlook, and the Dempsey Holder Safety Center. A visionary of the Public Art program, he convinced the Port District to place five art installations at city waterfront street ends.

He served two terms as Chairman of San Diego Board of the Regional Governments (SANDAG). In 2002, he was appointed Commissioner of the Unified Port District and elected Chairman in 2008. Bixler brought a modern Cruise Ship Terminal to Broadway Pier and in recognition, was named Commissioner Emeritus. Bixler worked closely with the U.S. International Boundary and Water Commission in the construction of the International Wastewater Treatment Plant and Ocean Outfall Pipeline, a project that significantly reduced

Barry Newman (1987)   William S. Conrad (1988)   Robert G. Scott (1989–90, 2005–07)   Michael J. Clark (1991, 2000–01)

Stanley F. Keniston (1992–93)   William Adair (1994–95)   Ann Southard Beard (1996–98)   Don Fine (1999, 2005)

Don Swall (2002)   Lawrence Wade (2004)   Robert G. Scott   Julie M. Walke (2008–2016)

contamination along coastal waters. In 2010 Bixler, along with his wife Sally, joined UBS Financial Services in San Diego.

BARRY NEWMAN (1987)

Newman graduated from the New York University School of Law in 1955. He joined the U.S. Army the same year and taught military justice at the Army Administration School in Fort Jackson, South Carolina. He later practiced law in New York and Cleveland and then began working in corporate banking with assignments in Los Angeles, New York, and Hartford, Connecticut. He joined Security Pacific Corporation in 1979. He chaired the Board of Trustees for the California Center for the Arts, was Vice-chair for San Diego's Metropolitan Wastewater Oversight Committee, member of the San Diego Mayor's Cultural Arts Task Force, and the Blue Ribbon Committee for the San Diego chapter of the American Red Cross. Newman was President of the San Diego County Civil Service Commission and also a Trustee for the downtown Gaslamp Quarter Theater Company. Newman passed away in 2010.

WILLIAM C. CONRAD (1988)

Banker Conrad had a distinguished career in San Diego finance, primarily as an executive with San Diego Trust & Savings Bank. A former Captain in the U.S. Marine Corps, he worked as a legal specialist for the Federal Deposit Insurance Corporation in Washington, D.C. He joined San Diego Trust in 1978 and served as Personnel Director and head of the Trust Group Division. In 1993, when San Diego Trust merged with First Interstate Bank, Conrad became Chairman of San Diego Trust Securities, Inc. Conrad was actively involved with the Junior Achievement. Conrad served on the Board at Coronado High School,

where he also taught a class in economics before he retired to Texas.

ROBERT G. SCOTT (1989–1990, 2005–07)

Born in Medford, Oregon, and raised in Portland, Scott earned his college degree in mechanical engineering at Oregon State University in 1964. He added a master's degree in systems management from the University of Southern California in 1979.

A San Diegan since 1977, Rob Scott ran his own engineering company: Building and Energy Systems. He retired in 2004 but remains active in the community and enjoys working with youth in organizations such as the YMCA, Boy Scouts of America, and Junior Achievement. Scott is also a fan of choral singing, and he retains a lifelong interest in restoring antique autos, which began at age fifteen with his first car, a 1927 Model T Ford.

MICHAEL J. CLARK (1991, 2000)

Clark was a prominent veterinarian and the owner of the San Diego Pet Hospital in Lemon Grove. Clark was the son of Griffith Clark, DVM, a 1962 graduate of the University of California, Davis. When Michael Clark graduated from UC Davis, he was the first son of a graduate veterinarian to graduate with the same degree from Davis. "Dr. Mike" was an active member of national, state, and local veterinary medical associations, he was appointed by California Governor Pete Wilson to the State Veterinary Medical Board in 1992. He served two four-year terms on the Board and was President from 1998 to 1999. Clark was also active in the Republican Party and served as a delegate to the National Convention in 1976. Clark passed away at the age of sixty-one in 2007.

STANLEY F. KENISTON (1992–93)

Architect Keniston is a graduate of Will C. Crawford High School in San Diego. Keniston attended the University of California, Berkeley, where he earned his B.A. degree in architecture in 1971. He has since directed his own architectural firm for over thirty years, specializing in building designs that integrate environmental and energy concerns. His professional affiliations include the American Institute of Architects, the American Solar Energy Society, and the Association of Energy Engineers.

Projects from Keniston Architects have won numerous awards and professional commendations. Honored architectural examples include the Julian Post Office—a popular new facility within a significant Historical District; the South Bay County Regional Center, Courts Expansion, in Chula Vista, which won an Orchid Award from the San Diego AIA; and the Visitor's Interpretive Center at the San Pasqual Battlefield State Historic Park, which combines energy efficiency with tri-cultural, historical sensitivity.

Active in San Diego community service, Keniston has served as Chair for Citizens for Clear Air Policy; member of the Board of Management, Human Development Services, YMCA; and Director for Citizen's Coordinate for Century Three.

WILLIAM ADAIR (1994–95)

Adair was for many years an executive for the Gildred Development Company of San Diego. Adair attended San Diego State College, where he earned a business marketing degree in 1964. An MBA at Santa Clara University followed in 1971. In the next decade, which Adair recalls as his "corporate years," he worked for Dow Chemical, Memorex, and Avery International.

Adair entered the real estate field in 1980 and earned professional CPM and CCIM degrees. He joined the Gildred Company in 1986 and rose to Executive Vice-president and Chief Operating Officer of the firm. Adair retired in 2007. Today, he is an avid golfer and active with the Fairbanks Country Club, where he serves on the Board of Directors.

ANN BEARD (1996–98)

Beard is the first woman President of the University Club elected in 1996. A graduate of Willamette University in Salem, Oregon, Ann Southard Beard is an internationally recognized diplomatic protocol consultant. For eight years Beard was the Chief of Protocol for the City of San Diego. She supervised the Mayor's International Affairs Board, the San Diego Consular Corps, and the International Sister Cities Program. Beard authored the official *Protocol Procedures Manual* for the city, and coordinated events such as the Summer Olympic Games, the America's Cup, and the APEC Foreign Ministers Conference. Beard welcomed over three thousand diplomats and dignitaries to the City. Beard is a graduate of LEAD San Diego, and serves on many community boards and committees. In 2002 Beard founded Protocol & Diplomacy International –Protocol Officers Association (PDI-POA) at the U.S. State Department in Washington, D.C., and received its "Spirit of Diplomacy" award in 2012. She retired from her consulting firm in 2013, and continues to serve as President of her family's oil-and-gas corporation.

DON FINE (1999, 2005)

Banker and realtor Fine was elected President of the University Club in 1999 and 2005. Fine earned his college degree in business and finance at the University of Dayton. He worked as a Bank

Examiner for the U.S. Treasury Department for three years. A second career in real estate followed. For twenty-five years, Fine worked for companies such as Loma Santa Fe and Willis Allen before forming his own mortgage company, until he retired in 2009. He also became a State Representative for the California Association of Realtors. He served in the Air National Guard and the Coast Guard Auxiliary. He was a founding member of the California Surf Museum in Oceanside. He has been an active member of the United Way and the North County chair of that social service agency. An avid sailor, Fine was a longtime member of the Coronado Cays Yacht Club. He passed away in 2014.

Lawrence Wade (2002, 2004)

Wade had a long career in California newspapers with the *San Francisco Chronicle*, the *Riverside Press Enterprise*, and the *San Marcos Outlook*. In 1982, Wade was recruited to publish the *Coronado Journal*. He later became a Manager for Great American Bank and then returned to newspapers in 1992 as the Editor of the *Coronado Eagle*. Wade served as President of the Coronado Rotary Club, a Director of the local Chamber of Commerce, and President of the Coronado Council of the Navy League. Wade authored a history book, *The Bridges of San Francisco Bay*, and hosted a weekly television show on archaeology called, "The Great Command." He was a member of a team of anthropologists from the University of California who identified the burial site of the Spanish California pioneer Juan Bautista de Anza. Larry Wade died at the age of eighty-three in 2012.

Julie M. Walke (2008–16)

English-born media consultant Julie Walke is only the second woman to be elected as President. She worked fifteen years at San Diego Trust & Savings Bank and as Assistant Vice President of Public Relations she managed the bank's one-hundredth-anniversary campaign. Founding Walke Communications Inc. in 1994, she has been a communications consultant for Fashion Valley Shopping Center and Belmont Village Senior Living in California and Arizona. She worked as an Associate Producer for two reality shows at Fox Television in Los Angeles, ESPN *Summer Games* and MTV's *Spring Break*. Walke received top awards from San Diego's Public Relations Society of America for crisis communications for the Blue Ribbon Committee, the Eva Irving Community Services Award for volunteerism and philanthropy and Best Government Campaign for City of Imperial Beach. Walke has penned articles for the *San Diego Business Journal* and other local publications. She authored a 2010 history title for Hugh O'Brien's Youth Leadership, *HOBY: The First Fifty Years*. In 2006, she authored, *Imperial Beach: A Pictorial History*.

CHAPTER FIVE

THE COLLEGE GRADUATE CLUB AND THE FOUNDING OF THE UNIVERSITY CLUB

Looking back, one might wonder when and why private clubs became important to the social fabric of the community, and if their relevancy has stayed the same throughout history. The roots of the private club started in 1896. It was then incorporated in 1909 as a male-only club, which changed to include female members in 1977. Most of the members transferred to the professionally managed Club, run by ClubCorp, in 1989, while the original corporation changed its mission toward philanthropic activities. ClubCorp, headquartered in Dallas, Texas, was owned by the Deadman family until being acquired by KSL. ClubCorp, now a KSL subsidiary, became a publicly traded company in September 2013 under the stock symbol of MYCC.

THE COLLEGE GRADUATE CLUB OF 1896

According to author Sylvia Flanigan who wrote "Social and Intellectual Affiliation: Formation and Growth of San Diego's University Club" for the *Journal of San Diego History* in 1985, "At the time of the Club's formation, the United States was experiencing a cultural revolution of higher learning and a growing middle class. The Civil War had ended thirty years earlier, and from coast to coast, schools of higher learning were being founded in specialties such as science, technology, architecture, agriculture, and mechanical arts and the formation of Graduate Schools took place.[1]

College Graduate Club minutes 1898. © San Diego History Center

OPPOSITE PAGE: University Club Lounge, circa 1917. © San Diego History Center

113

LEFT: Dr. Fred Baker and Dr. Charlotte Baker and their children. The Bakers were two founding members of the College Graduate Club who, in the beginning, opened their home or Dr. Charlotte Baker's office for meetings. © *San Diego History Center*

TOP RIGHT: Hazel Wood Waterman, circa 1880. © *San Diego History Center*

BOTTOM RIGHT: Kate O. Sessions in 1884 after her college graduation from University of California. A horticulturist and landscape architect, she was named the "Mother of Balboa Park" on September 22, 1935, for the extensive plantings throughout the park and in the areas surrounding the park. © *San Diego History Center*

This academic revolution spurred the intellectual identity of the country, separate from the rest of the world. "The generation produced after the Civil War was comprised in part of a group of young men and women of well-to-do, often eminent backgrounds. They were the first cluster of native intellectual aristocracy to appear. . . . Many sought nurturance in elite intellectual groups where they could socialize with others of similar birth and background and immerse themselves in the stimulating thoughts and ideas of their day.[2]

San Diego was also growing in the mid-nineteenth century. A busy port city, it was attractive to those who were tired of the cold East Coast climate. In 1855, the government built Point Loma Lighthouse to assist with maritime navigation. The population swelled to four thousand by 1872 and San Diego's "new town" scene was established with the expansive two-story Horton House and Plaza, which was reputed to be one of the largest in Southern California and designed to lure railroad development. By 1879, Frank Kimball's large amounts of land and money successfully enticed the Santa Fe Railroad. In 1881, the gas company set up its works and in 1882, and telephone service commenced with thirteen customers.[3]

San Diego's perfect and healthful climate, elite hotels, and growing business establishments were attracting many educated people to move out West. And, it was only natural that by the late-nineteenth century San Diego's growing citizenry was seeking intellectual identity.

The College Graduate Club was formed on October 8, 1896.[4] At the October 8 first meeting, twenty-one people, including thirteen women, gathered together to plan this organization which was to bring together people with academic degrees to discuss at regular monthly meetings the current topics of the day.[5]

Membership criteria included a university degree. Members (or graduates) kept a list of institutions in the official *Record.* At first, thirty-five colleges and universities were designated, most from Eastern-based Ivy League schools. Two years later, the list was expanded to forty-one schools and included two schools from California: Stanford University and University of California at Berkeley.

The College Graduate Club wrote a Constitution of eight articles, and established a specific meeting format. Each meeting started with a general business presentation followed by a reading of stories that appeared in the daily edition of the *San Diego Evening Tribune.*[6] The newspaper reading lasted only twenty minutes, after which the Chairman would choose a topic of discussion. Each member was limited to five minutes. The wives and husbands of members were designated as honorary members and were allowed to participate in discussions, but could not vote on business matters.

Membership was terminated if a member missed two consecutive meetings without an excuse.

Notable members from the original College Graduate Club were retired Senator David L. Withington, Judge Moses A. Luce, Kate O. Sessions, Dr. Fred Baker and his wife Dr. Charlotte Baker, Waldo and Hazel Waterman, Julius Wangenheim, Harry Morse, Mrs. Elisha Babcock, and Russell C. Allen.

COLLEGE GRADUATE CLUB: CHARTER MEMBERS		
R. C. Allen	Harvard	1880
Ruth G. Bagely	Michigan	1893
Mrs. Charles Barnes	Berkeley	1905
W. F. Bliss	Mt. Union	1885
	Berkeley	1893
Edith Cox	Berkeley	1901
Gordon Decker	Stanford	1898
Florence Dunbar	Stanford	1900
Dr. D. H. Elliot	Bucknell	1898
Harriet Godfrey	Berkeley	1895
Mrs. Kate Gridley	Stanford	1904
E. L. Hardy	Wisconsin	1893
Judge E. W. Hendricks	Brown	1871
Mary Hodge	Stanford	1903
Judge M. A. Luce	Hillsdale	1866
Duncan McKinnon	Stanford	1899
Miss Inez McQuiddy	Berkeley	1904
Mrs. Phillip Morse	Oberline	1876
Dr. Alice E. Pratt	Berkeley	1881
	Chicago	1897
Pete W. Ross		
Hugh T. Richards		
Kate O. Sessions	Berkeley	1881
Reverend S. L. Slaw	Princeton	1873
Judge W. A. Sloane	Iowa College	1877
Mrs. Sam Smith		
Dr. J. W. Stearns	Harvard	1860
A. H. Sweet	Baldwin	1883
Julius Wagenheim	Berkeley	1887
Mrs. Hazel W. Waterman	Berkeley	1887
Miss Emma Way		

CLUB CONSTITUTION

MEMBERSHIP COMMITTEE: Three people held elective office for one year. Responsibilities included maintaining the list of acceptable colleges and universities; receiving membership applications; checking the eligibility of the applicants; and reporting the names of prospective members to the Club to be voted upon. Members were elected by a 4/5 vote of those present at the regular meeting.

RECORDKEEPING: A secretary was assigned to keep records of Club proceedings and to notify members of the place and time of the meetings. Regular meetings were scheduled for every other Thursday evening at 7:30 p.m.

MEETINGS: Each meeting was to be presided over by an essayist who conducted the evening's discussion, and who then chose the essayist for the following meeting. No members would serve twice until a complete rotation of the membership roster had occurred.

The first meeting of the College Graduate Club was hosted by Dr. Charlotte Baker on Tuesday, October 22, 1896, by proxy, at her office, and provided extracts from Macaulay's *History of England*, taking up the subject of coinage.

Judge Morris Luce conducted the second meeting by reading an article entitled "Then and Now" where he took a look at the "good ole times" and compared them with modern conditions. The discussion focused on the condition and the advancement of women. Subsequent meetings emphasized topics such as Darwinism, race progress, universal peace, psychics, and the debate as to whether the higher education of women should differ in scope and direction from that of men, considering "certain recognized mental differences." Other topics discussed were manual training in schools, culture, and America, among others. The last topic of the

nineteenth century posed the question, "What should we do with our Girls?"[7]

The twentieth century brought forth new ideas for group discussion such as political reform, religion, minorities, labor, and the accomplishments of American men and women. Judge Morris Luce presided over a discussion of "Christianity and Imperialism." Member Waldo Waterman chaired a dialogue on "Municipal Ownership of National Monopolies." And Mrs. Hazel Waterman officiated a debate on "Organized Labor." Other themes included: "Charity and Progress," "Christ and the Rich," "Young Man," "War and Peace," "Selfishness and Evolution," and "The Increase in Lawlessness in the U.S."

In 1905 Mrs. Waterman presented a talk advocating the proposition that men under forty had accomplished practically all of the valuable work of the world. Additional discussions centered on women's inability to compose music, the Pure Food Law, and whether or not newspapers weaken our national fibre.[8]

In 1906 the College Graduate Club started to suffer a decline in interest and enthusiasm so, in May, the group renamed themselves the University Club in hope of attracting new members. They also decided to elect a president and a secretary-treasurer for an annual term. Club meetings were changed to bi-weekly and the executive committee was responsible for choosing the essayist. Dues were set at .50-cents per year. Unfortunately, even with the new name and amended rules, club disinterest prevailed with the termination of activities in 1907.[9]

UNIVERSITY CLUB

Drs Fred & Charlotte Baker

You are invited to attend the
Semi-Annual Dinner of the University Club
on Monday evening, March eleventh, at eight o'clock,
at "The Helix."
There will be an address by
Burt Estes Howard, A. M., Ph. D., of Los Angeles,
subject, "Democracy and Education,"
followed by a short discussion of the subject.
M. A. Luce, President,
Keating Block.

TO PREPARE PROPERLY, IT IS NECESSARY
THAT YOU NOTIFY THE PRESIDENT BEFORE
MARCH 9TH, STATING IF YOU CAN ATTEND
AND THE NUMBER OF TICKETS WANTED.
TICKETS, $1.25 PER PLATE

1907 Invitation to dinner prior to the Club's incorporation in 1909. © San Diego History Center

INCORPORATION OF THE UNIVERSITY CLUB IN 1909

According to Flanigan, "In late 1907, however, some male members of the moribund University Club joined with a group of men in the area who belonged to college fraternities and reorganized the University Club, which now only included male members and was open to all college alumni. This organization changed some of its original membership requirements and was directed by three prominent San Diegans: attorney Edgar A. Luce, architect William S. Hebbard, and Frank Von Tesmar, a teller for First National Bank. These men were also responsible for recruiting new members. The first meeting was held on December 8, 1908. Dr. H. P. Newman was elected as Chairman. A committee consisting of E. L. Hardy, Julius Wangenheim, Dr. D. D. Whendon, Hebbard, and Luce were responsible for its incorporation as a bona fide organization. The first President of the University Club, Russell C. Allen, an early member of the College Graduate Club, was elected."

Under the Articles of Incorporation on April 30, 1909, the University Club was to be a private corporation. The organization was to promote literature, art and general culture among the male members by establishing and maintaining a library, reading room, or gallery of art. It was to stimulate and encourage the desire to secure a higher education through the colleges and universities. It endeavored to foster and preserve college and university traditions. It planned to buy or lease a premises

PEOPLE WHO SIGNED THE ARTICLES OF INCORPORATION

The Articles of Incorporation were signed on April 30, 1909, and witnessed by:

Russell C. Allen	Frank Von Tesmar
W. S. Hebbard	Julius Wangenheim
C. E. Groesbeck	Henry P. Newman
Willard B. Thorpe	James E. Wadham
Edward L. Hardy	D. D. Whedon
Edgar A. Luce	

AY MORNING, MARCH 6, 1914

LAMBS AND GOATS DEFIED

✸✸✸   ✸✸✸   ✸✸✸   ✸✸✸

University Club Challenge Issued

Challenge issued by University Club to Cuyamaca Club Goats and Lambs.

To H. H. Jones,
President of the Cuyamaca Club:

Certain sounds resembling the bleating of lambs, believed to be emanating from within your walls, have so filled the atmosphere with vibrations of daring and combat that the dormant athletic prowess of the University Club has leaped forth in one harmonious declaration to play bold and 'cross bats when the signal is sounded.

We, who are possessed of nine real gambolers of the green whose hearts are still young, with the fire of youth, being skeptical of the skill of the arm-chair and pinochle artists wearing the colors of your clan, with the sanction of Manager MacKinnon and Captain Luce hereby send forth unto you our bold defi and challenge, to meet you when and where you will in the deadly combat of strikes and fouls.

Dated this 5th day of March, 1914.

UNIVERSITY CLUB OF SAN DIEGO,

By _Gordon L. Gray_
President.

By _Henry J. Bischoff_
Secretary.

New Aspirants Throw Down Gauntlet to Seasoned Athletes.

The die is cast. What Octavius threatened to do with Marc Antony when he marched into Egypt to punish the recreant Roman, the University Club baseball nine promise to hand the devoted Lambs and Goats of the Cuyamaca Club.

Captain Luce, of the University team, says his men are out daily now, getting hardened for the contest. He is delighted with the fact that each day a big black cat, with nine ebony kittens, sits in the grandstand and blinks at the players.

"Talk about mascots," said Luce. "Give me a black cat against all the bulls, bull-heifers, tame ducks, greased pigs and game chickens in the world, and the cat will win out every time.

"Our scouts have notified us that by spying upon the corral of the Goats and Lambs they have learned that the Cuyamaca Club bunch are disposed to force us into making a reputation before giving us battle. We respect the powerful aggregation of the Cuyamaca Club, and will bow to their edict.

"First, we wish to give them an opportunity to meet us on the diamond. If they refer us to their big brother of the Point Loma Golf Club then we will take on that party. What we want is baseball, and we are going to have it.

"'Sic semper tyrannus' is our battle cry."

for a Clubhouse where college and university men could acquire the ideals of higher education and where good fellowship could be developed.[10]

Early members included distinguished San Diegans such as Arthur Marston, Edgar A. Luce, S. T. Black, Reverend W. B. Thorp, Ernest E. White, Austin Fletcher, Captain A. P. Ballentine, U. S. Grant Jr., Dr. Fred Burnham, V. Hugo Klauber, George Marston, Duncan McKinnon, and Reverend Charles Spaulding. By 1911, there were 125 active members of the Club. By then, amendments to the bylaws specified that members needed to be college or university graduates from a specified group of schools. Exceptions were made for commissioned officers serving in the U.S. Army or Navy. Resident memberships were limited to 200 individuals with an initiation fee of $50. Nonresidents did not have an initiation fee but paid dues of $2.50 per month.

Rules were also published in 1911 that no member should tip employees or attendants in the service of the Club. Visits by ladies to the Clubhouse, except on stated occasions, was discouraged. However, if visits were deemed unavoidable, ladies were to be shown to the correspondence room. Dogs were not permitted in the (upstairs) residences.[11]

The reorganized University Club met in a rented mansion at the corner of Fourth and A Streets. There were ninety-two charter members when these quarters were first inhabited in 1909. A steak dinner cost thirty-five cents.

Baseball Game challenge between the members of the University Club and the Cuyamaca Club in 1914. *Courtesy of History Collection Gray, Cary Ames & Frye*

September 12th 1910

Dear Sir:

I have the honor to inform you of your election to resident membership in the University Club of San Diego.

Edward K. Lannon
Asst. Secretary

Membership Acceptance Note in 1910 to Gordon Gray who became University Club President in 1914. *Courtesy of History Collection Gray, Cary Ames & Frye*

UNIVERSITY CLUB
OF SAN DIEGO

The Annual Meeting and Charter Day Dinner will be held Friday Evening, January 16, 1914, at the University Club, at 6:30 o'clock.
Mr. Alfred Mosley, C.M.A., LL.D., will be the speaker of the evening.
Election of Officers and Directors for the ensuing year.
The Nominating Committee has nominated the following:

President . . . . Gordon L. Gray
Vice-President . . Dr. F. R. Burnham
Secretary . . . . C. O. Bullis
Treasurer . . . . P. V. Morgan

W. J. Gough	Wilmot Griffis	W. B. Gross
Hugo Klauber	Dr. A. D. Long	Duncan MacKinnon
	W. A. Sloane	

Please return the enclosed card promptly.

J. M. WARD, Secretary

Invitation to Annual Meeting and Dinner, January 16, 1914. *Courtesy of History Collection Gray, Cary Ames & Frye*

THE UNIVERSITY CLUB
Menu

Olives, Ripe or Green	.05
Pickles, Sweet or Sour	.05
Pickled Onions	.05
Swiss Cheese Sandwich	.10
Sardine Sandwich	.10
Lettuce Mayonnaise Sandwich	.10
Ham Sandwich, Sliced or Minced	.10
Chicken Sandwich, Sliced or Minced	.15
University Club Sandwich	.25

SPECIAL
SOUP
Cream of Tomato .05

MEAT *or* FISH
Roast Rib of Beef .25
Fillet of Sole, Tartar Sauce .25

VEGETABLES
Fried Sweet Potatoes .05
Sweet Corn .05
Spinach .05

DESSERT
Apple or Pumpkin Pie .05
Cup Custard .05

Baked Beans, Hot or Cold	.10
Creamed Tuna on Toast	.20
Creamed Chipped Beef and Poached Egg	.20
Two Eggs, any style	.20
Ham and Eggs	.25
Lamb Chops	.25
Pork Chops	.25
Individual Club Steak	.35
Cheese—American, Camembert or Roquefort, with crackers	.15
Certified Milk, per glass	.05
Tea, per pot	.05
Coffee, per cup	.05
Cocoa, per cup	.10
Mission beer, splits	.10
Special Claret Splits	.10

Cigars and Cigarettes.

*Potatoes, Bread and Butter
Served with All Meat or Fish Orders*

University Club Menu, 1914. *Courtesy of History Collection Gray, Cary Ames & Frye*

UNIVERSITY CLUB
OF SAN DIEGO

BALLOT
January 16, 1914

PRESIDENT
Gordon L. Gray *†

VICE PRESIDENT
Dr. F. R. Burnham *†

SECRETARY (Vote for one)
C. O. Bullis *
H. J. Bischoff †

TREASURER
P. V. Morgan *†

DIRECTORS (Vote for seven)
W. J. Gough *
Wilmot Griffis *
W. B. Gross *†
V. Hugo Klauber *
Dr. A. D. Long *†
Duncan MacKinnon *†
W. A. Sloane *†
W. B. Thorp †
J. F. Haight †
Dr. D. H. Elliott †

NOTE—
* Nominated by Nominating Committee.
† Nominated by ten members.

University Club Ballot, 1914. *Courtesy of History Collection Gray, Cary Ames & Frye*

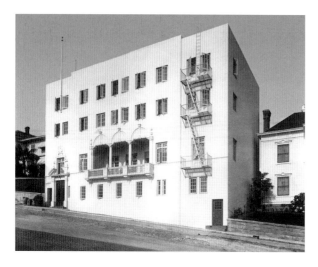

Architects H. S. Hebbert (University Club President 1911) and Carleton Winslow Jr. designed the four-story Spanish-style structure at 1333 Seventh Avenue, seen here in 1917. © *San Diego History Center*

University Club Lounge, 1926. © *San Diego History Center*

Dining Room interior, 1917. © *San Diego History Center*

Outdoor Patio at the University Club, 1917. © *San Diego History Center*

Member-architects William S. Hebbard and Carleton Winslow Sr. designed the first permanent Club location at 1333 Seventh Avenue. It was a four-story, Spanish-style structure that contained ground-floor offices, a reception desk, and a lounge to serve members with ladies or ladies who were alone. The upper two floors housed the residences that were bedrooms and suites for members and their guests. The cost of this building was $29,000.[12] The Sefton Library was established in accordance with the Club's stated purpose to promote literature, art, and general culture.[13]

By 1916, membership initiation fee was waived for active service military and clergymen. The annual dues for residents was raised to $30 and nonresidents were now required to pay $15. Any member in good standing could obtain a lifetime

University Club Dining Room, 1926. The painting on the wall (right) by L. Titus is called *Shadow Patterns*. It is still on exhibit as part of the 1909 University Club of San Diego Art Collection. © *San Diego History Center*

University Club Lounge, 1926. © *San Diego History Center*

University Club living quarters in 1926. © *San Diego History Center*

University Club of San Diego
Roster, 1926

Abbott, Clinton G.	Columbia Univ.	'03
Alberty, W. M.	Kansas Univ.	'17
Abendroth, C. W.	Purdue Univ.	'04
Allen, R. C.	Harvard	'80
Allen, Richard M.	Harvard	'11
Allen, Dr. W. E.	Univ. of Maryland	'01
Andrews, C. N.	Director Member	'16
Andrews, J. H.	Ohio Wesleyan	'90
Angier, Will	Univ. of California	'83
Arnold, Dr. Mott H.	Univ. of Illinois	'07
Allen, Maurice	Mass. Tech-Michigan	'11
Banks, Dr. Alfred E.	P. & S. Medical	'04
Bach, Ralph E.	Stanford	'14
Barney, L. W.	Univ. of Cal.	'10
Barclay, Henry A.	Univ. of Colorado	'06
Baxter, Dr. C. Pennel	Tufts College Medical	'14
Beach, Wm. D.	U. S. Military Academy	'79
Bell, Dwight D.	Univ. of Nebraska	'11
Benton, Dr. Culmer C.	Univ. of Pennsylvania	'14
Bischoff, Henry J.	Univ. of Kansas	'07
	Harvard Law	'12
Blondin, Dr. Edward A.	Washington Univ.	'19
Boal, John E.	Directors Member	'17
Butler, Dr. Edwin I.	Phila. Dental College	'08
Bretsch, Dr. G. H.	Univ. of Buffalo	'07
Bridges, A. S.	Directors Member	'17
Bullis, C. Orsmond	Ohio Wesleyan	'03
	Yale	'12
Burger, Dr. Thomas O.	Vanderbilt Univ.	'00
Burnham, Marston	Yale	'17
Byers, James C.	Univ .of Michigan	'00
Buchanan, Herbert F.	Univ. of Iowa	'18
Burton, Dr. F. A.	Univ. of Colorado	'06
Brown, Lawrence P.	Colo. School of Mines	'18
Brown, Dr. Charles	Univ. of Calif.	'17
Benton, D. C.	Princeton	'10
Busenburg, E. O.	Valparaiso, Ind.	'93

[13]

Roster of members, 1926. © *San Diego History Center*

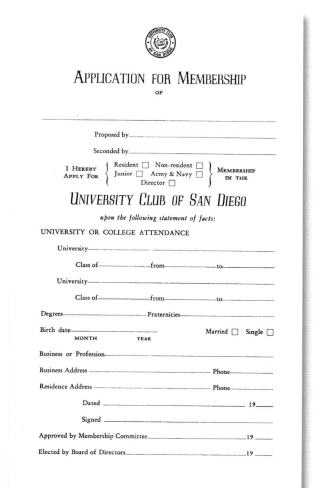

Membership application, circa 1947. © *San Diego History Center*

membership, with exemption from paying dues, for the remainder of his life for $60.[14]

The House Rules were updated in 1916 as well. The Clubhouse was open at 7 a.m. daily and closed at 12 p.m. after which admittance would be only to those who lived on the premises. No visitor or guest was allowed to introduce "strangers" to the Club. No more than two guests, by a member, were allowed at a time. Guests could pay for rooms at a cost of $1.50 per day. Private dinners could not include women, and no poker or gambling was allowed.[15]

A highlight of the University Club was its Friday noon luncheon programs. Participants were of "local and national eminence who reflected the broad gamut of human experience." Notable individuals included the following: American writer Hamlin Garland spoke in 1923 of "A Literary Summer in England"; actor Charles Coburn discussed "The Theater" in 1923; Edgar Hewitt, director of the San Diego Museum, spoke of "Recent Explorations in Western Asia" in 1923; Armand Jessop spoke about "Rambling in Africa" also in 1923; and Ali Kuli-Khan (Nabiled) Dowleh of Persia visited in April 1927 and spoke on "Persia's Contribution to the Western Culture."[16]

Performance poster, New Year's Eve 1929. © *San Diego History Center*

Performance poster, September 6, 1930. © *San Diego History Center*

Performance poster, January 19, 1928. *Photos by Bob Childs.* © *San Diego History Center*

THE CLUB IN THE 1940s

TOP LEFT: Club Library, 1947. The Alfred Mitchell painting on the wall (left) is still on exhibit as part of the 1909 University Club of San Diego Art Collection. *Interiors by W. & J. Sloane. Photography by Gene Lyle. © San Diego History Center*

TOP RIGHT: Main Dining Room, 1947. *Interiors by W. & J. Sloane. Photography by Gene Lyle. © San Diego History Center*

MIDDLE LEFT: Ladies Dining Room, 1947. *Interiors by W. & J. Sloane. Photography by Gene Lyle. © San Diego History Center*

MIDDLE RIGHT: Sitting Room, 1947. *Interiors by W.& J. Sloane. Photography by Gene Lyle. © San Diego History Center*

RIGHT: University Club Reception Room, circa 1960. *From the Hope Collection. © San Diego History Center*

THE CLUB IN THE 1950s AND 1960s

TOP: Exterior at Seventh Avenue and A Street, 1963. Note: The El Cortez building in the background on Seventh Avenue. © *San Diego History Center*

BOTTOM LEFT: Members and their guests enjoy the New Year's Eve party, 1953. *Ed Neil photographer, San Diego Union-Tribune Collection.* © *San Diego History Center*

BOTTOM RIGHT: New Year's Eve Party, 1954. Left to right: Dr. and Mrs. Walter R. Nickel, Mr. and Mrs. Books Crabtree, and Dr. and Mrs. Worth Martin. *Ed Neil photographer, San Diego Union-Tribune Collection.* © *San Diego History Center*

University Club china, circa 1960. *Courtesy of the 1909 University Club of San Diego Fine Arts Collection. Photo by ZackBenson.com*

The Club continued to offer a diverse and interesting range of programs. In 1942 Ed Fletcher presented "Our State Water Program" and Richard Pourade in 1945 talked about his experiences as a Washington correspondent. In 1960, Lute Mason of KFMB-TV discussed the 1960 Olympic Games in Rome. In 1961 Major General V. H. Krulak of the U.S. Marine Corps visited the Club and spoke about "The Place of the American Military Man in Our Country Today." Jack Kemp of the San Diego Chargers explained the team's arrival in 1961 along with showing a 1960 Chargers highlight reel. Jim Mulvaney of the San Diego Padres made a presentation called "They don't make Ball Players Like they Used To," which proves that some things never change! Also in 1964, Barry Goldwater Jr. of Arizona State University presented "A Victory We Shall Have"; while member architect Frank L. Hope, Jr. (University Club President 1956) educated members about the need for a $27-million bond issue for construction of the new football stadium that was expected to go to a citywide vote in November 1965. The stadium was built and is now known as Qualcomm Stadium. Politicians also gave presentations at the University Club. Programs of

note, including San Diego Mayor Pete Wilson who offered "Reflections on the System and Challenges to It" and Forty-first District Congressman Lionel Van Deerlin who presented "Gas Rationing Now" in 1973.[17]

By the late 1960s, Club members decided that they needed a new Clubhouse. The white, Spanish-style structure, designed by H. S. Hebbert (University Club President 1911), was rapidly deteriorating and the plaster inside and out was crumbling. Frank Hope was asked to design a new Clubhouse. He planned a three-story modern brick building that was erected on the corner of Seventh and A Streets. The old building was razed to make room for this structure. The new University Club, completed in November 1970, contained a gymnasium, sauna, steam room, and billiard room on the first floor. The second level held fifty parking spaces. The third or main club level housed the main dining groom and several private rooms as well as the club offices and library. There were no living quarters designed for this building. The Club financed the $1 million cost of the building by selling $300,000 worth of bonds to members and the rest was borrowed from a group of local financial institutions.[18]

For thirty years, the University Club of San Diego, Inc., was only open to male members. By, April 1975, the viewpoint towards women was changed by directors in part due to the growing Women's Movement but also because they needed new membership to help finance their new building (more about this in Chapter Three). The University Club of 1985 with its 650 members did not know that is was on the precipice of an entirely new journey.[19]

Inscription on Newell Post reads: "This was the newel post at the top of the stairway in the old club—1333 Seventh Avenue. (October 1916–October 1969). This post was salvaged due to activity and interest of Chandler Bach, Carl Davis, and 'Buddy' Durham. *Courtesy of the 1909 University Club of San Diego Fine Arts Collection. Photo by ZackBenson.com*

ENDNOTES

1. Sylvia K. Flanigan, "Social and Intellectual Affiliation: Formation and Growth of San Diego's University Club," *Journal of San Diego History*, Winter 1985, pp. 40–49.

2. Ibid.

3. Syd Love, *San Diego: Portrait of a Spectacular City*, San Diego Magazine Publishing Company, 1969, pp. 24–32.

4. Handwritten records of the first meeting of the College Graduate Club are contained in the *Record*, a lined hardbound notebook located at San Diego History Center Archives.

5. *The University Club of San Diego, Membership Roster, 1980–81.*

6. According to the online archive of California, the *San Diego Evening Tribune* was founded on December 2, 1895. It was one of three newspapers serving San Diego at that time. The other two were the *San Diego Union* and the *San Diego Sun.*

7. *Record*, pp. 15–22.

8. *Record*, pp. 26–42.

9. Information about the deteriorating membership; *The University Club of San Diego, Membership Roster, 1980–1981.*

10. Articles of Incorporation for the University Club of San Diego by the State of California July 6, 1909.

11. *The University Club of San Diego*, booklet, 1911, p. 11.

12. Carl Ritter, "University Club: 7th and A: Milestone For Future," *San Diego Union*, August 8, 1976, B-1.

13. Gail A. Burnett, "The University Club of San Diego—Past and Present," June 1989, p. 3.

14. *University Club of San Diego, 1916 Bylaws and House Rules with List of Members*, Jones Inc. Printers, 1916, pp. 17–18.

15. Sylvia K. Flanigan, "Social and Intellectual Affiliation: Formation and Growth of San Diego's University Club," *Journal of San Diego History*, Winter 1985, pp. 46–47.

16. *Friday Programs, The University Club of San Diego*, Volume 1 (1922–1960) hardbound.

17. Sylvia K. Flanigan, "Social and Intellectual Affiliation: Formation and Growth of San Diego's University Club," *Journal of San Diego History*, Winter 1985, p. 48.

18. "University Club Dedicates a New Home," *San Diego Union*, November 20, 1970, p. 3.

19. Sylvia K. Flanigan, "Social and Intellectual Affiliation: Formation and Growth of San Diego's University Club," *Journal of San Diego History*, Winter 1985, p. 48.

ABOUT THE AUTHORS

English-born media consultant **Julie M. Walke** founded Walke Communications Inc. (WalkePR) in 1994. The company specializes in media relations, crisis communications, photography, and the written word. She has received top awards from the Public Relations Society of America (PRSA) for crisis communications for the Blue Ribbon Committee of the American Red Cross; the Eva Irving Community Services Award for volunteerism and philanthropy; and the Best Government Campaign for City of Imperial Beach. She is only the second woman to be elected as President of the University Club of San Diego.

Prior to WalkePR, Walke was Assistant Vice President of Public Relations at San Diego Trust & Savings Bank where she managed the Bank's 100th Anniversary campaign. She has also worked as an Associate Producer for two reality shows at Fox Television in Los Angeles, ESPN *Summer Games* and MTV's *Spring Break*.

Walke has penned articles for the *San Diego Business Journal* and other San Diego publications. She has authored three titles with Donning Company Publishers—*A Pictorial History of the University Club of San Diego* (2014); *Hugh O'Brian Youth Leadership, HOBY: The First Fifty Years* (2010), and *Imperial Beach: A Pictorial History* (2006). Ms. Walke has a Bachelor's Degree of Fine Arts in Interior Design. She is a member of the San Diego Press Club, Mingei International Museum, Museum of Contemporary Art San Diego (MCASD), and the Ilan Leal Foundation. Her personal goal is to write about the life and work of Julia Morgan.

RICHARD W. CRAWFORD is the Supervisor of Special Collections at the San Diego Public Library. He is the former Archives Director at the San Diego Historical Society, where he also edited the *Journal of San Diego History* for nine years. Born in Long Beach, he has been a San Diegan since 1973. He has degrees in history (San Diego State University) and library science (San Jose State University). As a historian and archivist, he has written extensively on local history, including the books *Stranger Than Fiction: Vignettes of San Diego History, The Way We Were in San Diego*, and the recently published *San Diego Yesterday*.

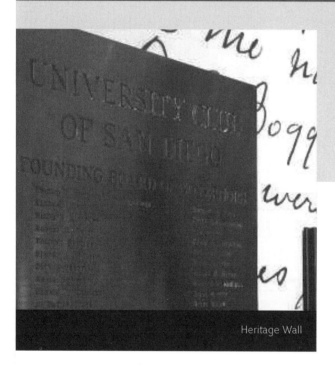

Heritage Wall

THEN

Under the Articles of Incorporation of 1909, the University Club was to be a private corporation. The organization was created to promote literature, art, and general culture among the Members by establishing and maintaining a library, reading room or gallery of art. It was created to stimulate and encourage 'young men' to secure a higher education through colleges and universities. The Club endeavored to foster and preserve college and university traditions. The corporation planned to purchase or lease premises for a clubhouse where college and university men could acquire ideals of higher education and where good fellowship could be developed.

NOW

Today, the Club continues to be a vehicle for Members to enjoy cultural events (Club Night at the Opera coming up May 17), participate in intellectual/business conversations (Distinguished Speaker Series the last Friday of each month) and support higher education through the Club's Lamp of Learning Scholarship foundation. The Club now serves over 1,700 Members (2,900 individuals) and is governed by a Board of Directors with Doug Wilson, acting Chairman of the Board.

1916: San Diego Zoo Opens

1916 San Diego Zoo created. Dr. Harry Wegeforth brings the San Diego Zoo into being when animals imported for the Panama-California Exposition are quarantined and not allowed to leave. He's reported to have exclaimed to his brother, Paul, "Wouldn't it be wonderful if we had a zoo?" He puts a notice in the newspaper, asking for support.

1919 United States Navy decides to make San Diego Bay home base for the Pacific Fleet.

1927 Charles Lindbergh completes historic flight

1927 Lindbergh completes his historic solo nonstop flight from New York to Paris May 20-21.

1928 San Diego Historical Society incorporated, with George White Marston as its founder and first president.

1800	1900	1910	1920

Spring is in full swing at the University Club. The calendar is chock-full of new and exciting events, and we are thrilled to see Members using their Club more diversely than ever before. Watching the game. Entertaining. Working. Negotiating. Relaxing. Dining. Networking. Celebrating. As the summer months near, the Club is pulsating with a dynamic energy that we've never before felt.

With all that's happening, have you taken some time out to roam the halls and explore some of the history and progression of San Diego and The University Club? If you haven't had the chance to check out the heritage wall, read on to discover how our long past, dating back to the 1890s, intertwines with that of America's Finest City.

1896 College Graduate Club created by 21 individuals, including 13 women, to bring together persons with academic degrees to discuss current topics of the day at regular monthly meetings. This College Graduate Club later evolves into the University Club.

1909 University Club founded.
"The University Club is to be a private corporation ... to promote literature, art and culture amongst Members ... to encourage the importance of education ... to preserve University traditions ... and to establish a clubhouse where good fellowship can be developed among Members," from the Articles of Incorporation of 1909. The reorganized University Club meets in a rented mansion at the corner of Fourth and A Streets. There are 92 charter members, and a steak dinner at this establishment costs 35 cents.

1911 The University Club rules were published in 1911. Visits of ladies to the club house, except on stated occasions, were discouraged. But "if the visits happened to be unavoidable, the ladies should be shown to the correspondence room."

1916 University Club establishes first Clubhouse. A four-story Spanish-style structure is designed by Member architects, William S. Hebbard and Carleton Winslow Sr., and built at 1333 Seventh Ave. The ground floor contained the offices, reception desk and a lounge to serve Members with ladies or ladies alone. The upper two floors house bedrooms and suites for Members and guests. The cost for this building is estimated at $29,000.

1919 University Club Highlights Friday Luncheon Forums highlighting various guests and topics over the years

1911: Ladies are discouraged from visiting the clubhouse.